"Will It Fly?"

The Idea Tester

Carla Langhorst

Order this book online at www.trafford.com
or email orders@trafford.com

Most Trafford titles are also available at major online book retailers.

© Copyright 2009 Carla Langhorst.
Cover photograph taken by Iulia Jurgea.
Author photograph taken by Pink Pearl Images.
All images are from Graphics Factory.
Copyediting by Sarah Moore.

Note for Librarians: A cataloguing record for this book is available from Library and Archives Canada at www.collectionscanada.ca/amicus/index-e.html

Printed in Victoria, BC, Canada.

ISBN: 978-1-4269-1307-5

We at Trafford believe that it is the responsibility of us all, as both individuals and corporations, to make choices that are environmentally and socially sound. You, in turn, are supporting this responsible conduct each time you purchase a Trafford book, or make use of our publishing services. To find out how you are helping, please visit www.trafford.com/responsiblepublishing.html

Our mission is to efficiently provide the world's finest, most comprehensive book publishing service, enabling every author to experience success. To find out how to publish your book, your way, and have it available worldwide, visit us online at www.trafford.com

Trafford rev. 6/19/2009

 www.trafford.com

North America & international
toll-free: 1 888 232 4444 (USA & Canada)
phone: 250 383 6864 ♦ fax: 250 383 6804 ♦ email: info@trafford.com

The United Kingdom & Europe
phone: +44 (0)1865 487 395 ♦ local rate: 0845 230 9601
facsimile: +44 (0)1865 481 507 ♦ email: info.uk@trafford.com

TABLE OF CONTENTS

DISCLAIMER

Business is an art rather than a science. There are no guarantees. The ideas contained in this book are generalizations based on existing business best practices. It is impossible for a single book to take into consideration every scenario which could result in an idea being a success or a failure.

This book can test:

- New businesses
- New services
- New products
- Any idea that requires an investment of time or money

Although the Idea Tester may indicate that your idea is feasible, significant market research is required prior to moving forward with a venture. Any action taken based on information found in this book is taken at the sole risk of the individual. Additional business advice regarding the specific opportunity should be sought out.

Due diligence is the responsibility of the entrepreneur.

ACKNOWLEDGMENTS

People will help you when you least expect it. I'm still shocked at the support I was given from avenues I had not expected.

Thank you to all of my friends and family who have put up with me, have given me second homes, have been supportive no matter what I'm thinking of doing that day. Some have even thanked me for turning to them for help – and that made me feel a lot better about asking for it!

"Thank you!"

CHAPTER ONE:
WHAT'S AN IDEA TESTER?

Introduction

So, you want to own your own business. Whether it's a hair salon, coffee shop, dog trimming service, an import business, accounting firm, or any other business idea – you need to test your idea.

Your new idea is fabulous and everyone else thinks so too. You don't know where to start, but you know that you have to start somewhere.

Here's the ideal place!

The Idea Tester will help you figure out if your idea will fly. Business plans are tedious and complex.[1] Not everyone has spent thousands of dollars on business degrees, but anyone can come up with great ideas. Entrepreneurs can end up more confused after writing a plan than

---

1   Business plans are the traditional documents required by a bank, an angel investor, or a venture capitalist in order to give start-up investment money. Even if an entrepreneur is not looking for funding, it is recommended that he or she have a written business plan to organize thoughts and commit plans to paper. A business plan is always being updated as the company grows and changes directions. The typical content of a business plan includes an executive summary, an outline of the offering, the sales projections, a marketing plan, an operations plan, a human resources plan, an exit strategy, a growth strategy, and the financial details for the first three to five years.

before they started. This Idea Tester is designed to be fast and to speak your language. It helps to clearly define your idea and gets you on your way to starting your business **tomorrow**.

In another sense, this book is like a business degree in a box. The simplified models have been selected from hundreds used by consultants and business students every day. Take advantage of these tools and put yourself on a level playing field without paying the tuition and taking the financial hit.

There are two challenges an entrepreneur may face when starting a new business:

1.   He or she has a million-dollar idea, but needs to start up the company while completing the business plan required for future funding.

2.   He or she has too many ideas and is unable to focus.

The Idea Tester solves these problems by testing the idea quickly and creating a framework to move the idea forward tomorrow.

CHALLENGE #1: A MILLION-DOLLAR IDEA

Have a million-dollar idea for a business?

Do you really know what you're getting into?

How long does it take to write a solid business plan – one that will secure the money which you'll eventually need from family and friends, angel investors, or venture capitalists?[2,3] Experts say that such a plan normally takes two to four months of full-time effort, depending on the maturity of your idea and the complexity of the business.

How much does this normally cost? It could cost anywhere from $3,000 to $20,000 with professional help, but that doesn't always take into account your own time (which is still worth something to most of us).

Further, in order to get the financial support for a million-dollar idea from a venture capitalist or an angel investor (and most definitely a bank), you will usually be required to put your own money into the execution of the idea. This means that you'll need to have some equity in the idea and have created something tangible before loans will be considered. However, since your business plan would still be in the development stage, you would lack a concrete action plan, and may be hesitant to make that personal financial investment. Time is money.

---

2 An angel investor is a specific type of investment company which works with grass-roots start-up companies. These investors require a higher return on investment and some level of controlling interest in the company. Further, they act as business advisors to the founders. They are called angel investors as it is a blessing to have them and sometimes a miracle to find them.

3 Venture capitalists are similar to angel investors but deal with companies which are slightly more developed. Usually the entrepreneur must have already invested a significant amount of time and money in the idea.

CHALLENGE #2: A MILLION DIFFERENT IDEAS

Have a million different ideas and find it difficult to focus?

Which idea is best for you?

One of the most common reasons why people fail in developing their own businesses is that they have **too many things on their plates**. We all hear about entrepreneurs who work sixty to eighty hours a week to start a new business. What would happen if they were trying two ideas or even three at the same time? The math would dictate that they would be working 180 hours to 240 a week! This is highly impractical, given the constraint of 168 hours in a week (24 hours x 7 days = 168 hours).

My "Ah-ha!" Moment

Graduating during one of the biggest economic downturns in history (and definitely in my lifetime), turned out to be one of my biggest opportunities. When you're employed, a big obstacle stands in the way of starting your own business. It's called a **job**.

A month into my job search, I became tired of telling people that I was unemployed. Then it dawned on me – "Ah-ha!" – that the amount of time I needed to re-establish my network, search job boards, and constantly update my resume and cover letter could be more effectively utilized looking for customers instead. I was attending networking events already! And the participants there would rather have spoken to an entrepreneur than an unemployed graduate.

At networking events, I started answering questions differently, telling people that I was employed through my own consulting firm; unfortunately, with the downturn in the economy, I didn't have many customers.

By changing my focus, one problem was removed: there was no need to go through the stress and potential loss of opportunity involved in leaving a job in favour of starting a business. Instead of looking for an employer, I would spend my time looking for customers!

However, a second problem quickly crept up. If I was self-employed, what was I selling? Examining my skills, past experience and passion led me in all sorts of directions. In the end, I had three to five business plans that I'd have to develop in order to move forward. If you do the math, that would take me nine to fifteen months! With that kind of math, I was more likely to succeed by putting all the ideas on a dartboard and letting the dart decide. At least then I could focus my energy and have a concrete plan in a reasonable time frame!

In the end, it came down to a little help from a friend, now my legal "muse." She was also unemployed, which was happening to a lot of good people, and was mulling over the same question as I: keep looking for an employer or start looking for customers?

5

With five entrepreneurship courses and a business degree tucked nicely behind me, I decided that I should sit down and help her with a business plan. In addition to being one of my closest friends, she's also a paralegal, and you never know when her help might come in handy!

Within the first five minutes and three sips of coffee, I realized that the traditional business plan format wasn't going to work for her. She didn't need funding immediately. (Besides, with the economic downturn, banks were a little tighter on lending.) What she needed was a confidence boost, to feel that success was not only possible, but probable. This would give her the momentum she needed to get started.

So, we crunched the numbers and realized that based on her salary expectations, she needed surprisingly few clients for success with an ongoing, self-sustained business. We developed a strategy to work with these numbers and an action plan for her to start the very next day. Two hours and a drained cup each later, we parted ways. Within three weeks, she had her first corporate client, giving her enough business to sustain herself.

That day in the coffee shop, two plans were hatched – her paralegal business, and this book.

"Ah-ha!"

The Problem with Traditional Business Plans

Writing a business plan is complex and time consuming; it feels like a waste of time, as it's constantly being updated.

"Too much work!"

The Solution

The solution is a quick and easy way to test your business ideas.

Well folks... Here it is! Quick, easy, painless.

1. Outline your idea.

2. See if the numbers make sense.

3. See if the idea fits your desired lifestyle.

Where these three aspects of a business idea overlap, you will find success.

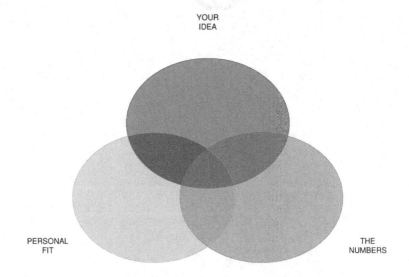

Figure 1: The Solution

Quick? Yes! This is a litmus test for your idea. Don't spend days, weeks, or months doing research. At this point, the test only asks that you have a basic idea of costs and of your business model. The nice thing is that it's so fast, you can test **many** different business models in the same time it would previously have taken to totally vet one idea.

Easy? Yes! You are getting all the best concepts to start your own business on the easiest terms. I've done extensive testing with people who have never taken a business course, have been retired for over fifteen years, or have never had a full-time job. That being said, I've also had feedback from an entrepreneurship professor, a financial planner, a banker, MBA graduates, and serial entrepreneurs. This stuff is tested and true!

How Does It Work?

The entire process is designed to systematically tune your idea, so that it both is feasible and meets your expectations. Some ideas can be disposed of in minutes, since the idea has to pass a test at each stage in order to move to the next. The process is outlined below in Table A.

Table A   The Idea Tester Framework

Test Stage Weighting	Stage Sections	Suggested Time Commitment
Your Idea (25%)	Fulfilling a Need	25%
	Your Offering	20%
	Differentiation	50%
	Test	5%
	Total	*100%*
The Numbers (35%)	Cost of Being In Business	50%
	Profit Margin	30%
	Break-Even Point	10%
	Test	10%
	Total	*100%*
Personal Fit (40%)	Your Passion	1%
	Self-Analysis	30%
	Salary Expectations	14%
	Work-Life Balance	50%
	Test	5%
	Total	*100%*

If your idea passes the previous test stage, then you invest more time in it. Once it has been evaluated against all three tests, you can then consider moving forward or doing more research to support your initial thoughts. If you make it through this process, you should be ready to get started the next day!

The entire breakdown for the Idea Tester in Table A is based on a percentage of time. The total time to evaluate an idea will vary from one idea to the next, based on how much research you have done and how much you have formulated the concept. The key is to optimize your time. Ensure that you only begin investing more time into the idea if it passes the test.

Stage 1: Your Idea

The first step is ensuring that the idea meets a genuine need. If there is **no need**, customers will not be willing to spend any money. Without a need, there is **no market,** and consequently, **no business**. If, at the end of this test stage, you have determined that the idea does not fulfill a need, move on to the next idea. If the idea does not fly, do not pass go, as you will **not** make a million dollars.

A clear example is a new piece of exercise equipment to strengthen the big toe. This idea does not satisfy a need, so there is no point in crunching the numbers. Without fulfilling a genuine need, there is no need to move to the next test stage.

Stage 2: The Numbers

Test the numbers. There is no point considering this idea further if the numbers don't work. **Stop.** OR, if you really love it, continue doing it as a hobby. Or perhaps create a not-for-profit business. Good entrepreneurs are not attached to their ideas; instead, they view them critically, based on the numbers.

If the numbers aren't showing a profit, there is no need to move forward to the personal fit test. It doesn't make sense to mix a bad idea with your lifestyle.

Stage 3: Personal Fit

Figure out if you can afford the time and money on a personal level to move this idea forward. It's possible that the idea is feasible, but not in harmony with your lifestyle. Maybe you can't afford the risk, perhaps it isn't your passion, or perchance you don't want to work weekends. Whatever it is, move on to a different idea. Or wait until your personal circumstances change. Or convince someone else to run with your idea. You need to determine whether the idea is a good fit for **you**.

Have five ideas? Use the Idea Tester on them all. Does one idea look easier to implement? Does one idea appear to have more potential in the long run? Choose the idea that best suits your lifestyle. If you are having a hard time choosing between a few ideas, use the niche marketing tool in Chapter Five to help you decide.

Then... Focus.

Business plans are important and almost all business books suggest having one. The old saying, "If you fail to plan, you plan to fail," is true. Just as important – a great plan with good implementation is less successful than a good plan with great implementation. If the business idea has gone through the Idea Tester, you'll have greater confidence in your idea, and a plan which will generate momentum. With other unproductive ideas discarded, you'll be able to focus, improving your chance of successful implementation.

The Ground Rules

The following are a few ground rules you need to know before moving forward.

1. **Be honest**

   You are only hurting yourself if you're not.

2. **Weigh the cost of your time against the benefit gained from research in making a decision**

   It takes time to research information. The time-cost investment to be 100% accurate often outweighs the benefit of making a marginally better decision with marginally better information. This balance must be carefully weighed. Examples where you might have to weigh the time-cost versus the benefit of research are listed below in Table B.

Table B   Time-Cost versus the Benefit of Research in Decision Making

If you need to...	Time-Cost	Benefit
Confirm fundamental assumptions about your idea...do it!	There are two to three things that need to be validated and there are a few people who have the concrete answers.	You find out whether or not your whole idea is a waste of time up front.
Validate your specific sales projections... wait!	Hundreds, if not thousands, of people need to be asked or a market test has to be organized.	You can't be 100% sure your offering will be successful until you launch. This investment will only marginally increase your confidence. Save it for the business plan.

Identify your major cost drivers... do it!	There are only a few.	If your estimates are off, even by a bit, your entire model will be affected.
Specify all of your costs... wait!	There are many and they vary in size.	Your estimates are going to be higher and lower, and you will inevitably miss costs in your original estimation. Being picky doesn't matter for minor expenses.

3. Don't flog a dead horse

If you fail a test and can't see a way around it, stop wasting your time. Remember that time is money, and if there is no foreseeable benefit to spending the time, don't!

4. Don't do this test in a vacuum

There are always exceptions. This test is not a fail-safe plan. Continue to use your network, including friends and family, as a sounding board for ideas.

5. Proceed with developing a business plan

A business plan is still necessary for a start-up business. You'll need it to apply for funding, to communicate your idea, to commit yourself to a structure, and to go through the planning process. However, spend this time only after the idea is tested!

6. Have fun!

Quick & Easy Summary: What's an Idea Tester?

- Entrepreneurs need an Idea Tester before writing a business plan.

- This procedure is quick, since you only invest time in the idea if it has passed previous test stage. Otherwise, **stop**!

- This procedure is easy, as the business models have been simplified and selected from hundreds.

- Business plans are still important to help an entrepreneur focus and raise the necessary capital, but only after completing the Idea Tester.

CHAPTER TWO:
YOUR IDEA

The First Test Stage

Welcome to the first stage in testing your idea. Recall from Table A that this stage is given a 25% weighting in the overall testing framework. As a reminder of how much time to commit to each section of this stage, part of Table A has been replicated below.

Table C   Your Idea Framework

Test Stage Weighting	Stage Sections	Suggested Time Commitment
Your Idea (25%)	Fulfilling a Need	25%
	Your Offering	20%
	Differentiation	50%
	Test	5%
	Total	100%

At this point, it's assumed that you have an idea in mind. **However, it does not have to be 100% planned out.** What is your basic concept?

Your concept should include:

1. Your Basic Product/Service

The basic product/service should be just that: basic. You don't have to know all of the accessorial services, or how the customer will be invoiced. What is the basic idea?

2. The Supporting Business Model

The business model is how the product or service is delivered. You need to know whether you are planning to have a storefront or direct marketing business, a webpage-based or trade-show-based business. Your business model will determine all of the costs, the total offering you are able to provide and what differentiates your business from the competition. If you have several different business models, you should run each through the Idea Tester.

This chapter outlines the first test stage. It will help you to define the specific (and genuine) need that you are satisfying, and results in a clear understanding of your offering and how it fulfills that need. Further, it will help you to identify what is unique about your offering compared with the competition; otherwise, customers have no reason to switch over.

Putting your concept down on paper will ensure that your idea is clear. Once you are able to clearly articulate the need, the product concept and what makes it unique, you will have developed your thirty-second elevator pitch.[4] Use Form 1, below, to capture these three components of your idea. You can use this communication framework when pitching the idea to friends, investors, customers – pretty much anyone!

---

4 A thirty-second elevator pitch is your best form of promotion. All of those people who claim that their only advertising is word-of-mouth (WOM) have a clear, concise way to communicate their ideas to others. Time is money. People retain only two to three pieces of information from a given conversation. So, make sure that your pitch is brief and that your audience will remember the pertinent details. If you can't clearly articulate your idea in thirty seconds (or less!), then your message will be lost. If your customers don't understand what you offer, they will not buy from you.

Form 1   Idea Outline

Idea Component	Question	Answer
The Need	What is the specific customer need your offering will serve?	
Your Offering	What is the complete overview of your offering?	
Differentiation	What makes your offering unique versus the competition?	

That's pretty easy!

Spending time on this section is crucial. The concept you develop here will carry through the rest of the Idea Tester and will eventually form the foundation of your marketing campaign. The strength and clarity of your concept will ultimately determine the success of your business. In fact, if your idea doesn't pass this section of the Idea Tester, you shouldn't move on to the next section.

So, let's do it right! And be honest.

Fulfilling a Need

Start with the need. Many inventors fall in love with a new concept, feature or product that they have developed. However, successful entrepreneurs don't start with the solution; rather, they start with the problem.

Ask yourself, Is there truly a need to be serviced here? The most common analogy is that of a customer purchasing a drill to assemble a piece of furniture. In this case, the customer is actually purchasing the holes required for assembly. The need to be fulfilled here is the not the drill, but the hole. It is important to understand your customer's true need.

This same concept can be illustrated through many different examples:

- You don't actually need a cup of coffee – rather, you need to stay awake.
- You don't actually need a towel – you need to get dry.
- You don't actually need a haircut – you need to look your best.
- You don't actually need small claims representation – you need remuneration.
- You don't actually need a hammer – you need to hang a picture to improve your home.

"Don't hurt yourself looking for the need – it should be obvious!"

Some products satisfy multiple needs for one person. And, conversely, many alternatives (or substitutes) can satisfy the same need for different people. The first example above concerning coffee is an excellent example of this.

- Some people don't need the cup of coffee; they just need to wake up. A shower might help.
- Other people don't need the cup of coffee; rather, they are cold and want to warm up. A cup of hot water would do.
- You don't need the cup of coffee; you want the aroma and warmth to add to a shared moment with a loved one. Hot chocolate or tea might work.
- Charles doesn't need the cup of coffee; he thinks that having coffee available to guests makes him a good host. He could serve plenty of other things for that!

You get the point.

By starting with a clearly defined need, you will be able to understand the true value that you are offering a customer. This has a side benefit: by understanding the true value of a product to your customer, you are better able to determine a customer's willingness-to-pay (WTP).[5] This will help you determine if there is a market for your product.

Time Tip: You don't have to survey one hundred people to determine whether or not there is a need for your offering. Ask ten. If one of those ten questions the need for your offering, ask another ten. If again only one person questions the need for your offering, you're pretty safe to move forward.

---

5 A willingness-to-pay (WTP) is responsible for all of the product varieties out there! If the product is slightly different due to branding, additional services, or slightly different features, the price point can change dramatically. Why can Prada or Gucci charge 1000% more than a no-name manufacturer for a purse with only marginally better quality (or none at all)? The WTP factor is extremely important. If your customers aren't willing to pay a specific price for what you are offering, you are out of business. If the customers are willing to pay far more than you are charging, you may be leaving money on the table.

Quick & Easy Summary: Fulfilling a Need

- Start with a need, **not** a product, service, feature, or type of technology.

- The same offering satisfies different needs for different customers.

- An offering can sometimes satisfy more than one customer need; the more needs it satisfies, the more value it creates.

Your Offering

Once the need has been clearly established, you develop an offering to meet that need in the best fashion possible. This is the most effective basis for marketable ideas.

Why is it called an "offering"?

In today's competitive business environment, it is unlikely that a business is fulfilling a customer need 100% through a product, or 100% through a service. More often than not, it is a combination. In fact, if you believe that you can meet a customer's need 100% through one method or another, think again.

A great example is a stuffed animal, traditionally viewed only as a product. However, WebKinz used the World Wide Web to create an accompanying service by allowing children to name and play with their stuffed animal characters online. This additional service added value to the WebKinz physical product and supported a premium price point.

Conversely, companies are trying to make their services more tangible. By coupling a product with a service, companies are creating a physical presence and being recalled more readily by the customer. The physical presence adds value, which helps you to win and retain customers (and may even allow you to charge more!).

The more your offering fulfills a customer's need, the less chance that a substitute offering or a competitor will be able to push you out of the market.

Some of the questions you should be thinking about in this section:

- What is your product/service?
- Does your product/service meet the need you previously identified?
- Does it meet the need completely or are additional products/services necessary?
- Are you also providing these products/services?

- Is there a different offering on the market which fulfills the need more completely than yours?
- If so, does your product/service offer the customer more value?[6]

Let's go through these questions with two different examples.

Table D Product and Service Offerings

Questions	Product Example	Service Example
What is the need?	Get Dry Anywhere	Look Good
What is your product/service?	Towel	Hairdresser
Does your product/service meet the need?	Dries the body and is portable	Guarantees that the customer will look good
Does it meet the need fully?	Product does not dry the hair; difficult to take everywhere after it is wet; bulky	Service does not include matters concerning clothing, make-up, accessories, self-esteem
Are you providing extra products/services?	Hair cap? Tips on drying procedures on web page? Quick drying towels? Different sizes for portability? Thinner?	Are other tips given? Make-up; colour advice; wardrobe consulting; massage; the complete package?
Is there another offering satisfying the need more completely?	Hair dryer Travel towel	Salon Spa

---

6 Value is the difference between the base cost of your product and a customer's willingness-to-pay. This difference is the value that your offering brings to the customer. If your customers aren't willing to pay more than your product's cost, then you haven't brought value to them and will not be in business for long (if at all!).

Is your offering able to offer better value?	Dries faster than a blow dryer; warmer and softer than a travel towel	Give a massage while asking about hair goals; take before and after pictures; give a free gift, such as nail polish, hair products to help maintain hair

By going through these questions about the offering and the competition, you will be able to vet out your offering. You will understand the value that you bring to customers, their willingness-to-pay, and your cost for that offering. Both your price and costs will be required in the next chapter.

Time Tip: *Knowing EVERY detail doesn't matter at this point! Just have the general idea and offering laid out. The details can be considered after you have determined that the idea is worth investing your time. The key is to ensure that your idea is sufficiently fleshed out – that it satisfies the need and generates a willingness-to-pay based on value. That's it! If you have reached that point, move on.*

Quick & Easy Summary: Offering

- Offerings are rarely 100% a product or 100% a service. More often, they are a combination of the two.

- The more an offering completely satisfies a customer's need, the better.

Differentiation

Differentiation means that your offering is set apart from the competition. There are four tasks to complete to ensure that your offering is genuinely unique:

1. Identify your competition.

2. Understand your competitors' strengths and weaknesses.

3. Create an offering that is different and adds value in a way the competition doesn't. This difference **must be important** to the customer.

4. Ensure that it's difficult for your competition to duplicate this difference.

1. Identify Your Competition

Before you can determine if your offering is different and better than your competitors' offerings, you have to acknowledge that there is competition and that doing business is a battle. If you believe that you don't have any competition and that your business is one of a kind – think again! Even if your offering is unique, there are other ways that the need is currently being fulfilled that you should identify.

Who are your competitors?

It's important to pinpoint who is in the playing field and how they are playing. You don't want to be concerned about everyone and yet you don't want to zero-in on one or two competitors. The former is too broad and will not allow you to focus, while the latter is too focused and may cause you to overlook a fierce competitor before it is too late.

One example is that of a water park. If the park owner only considered other water parks as the main competition, he or she would not take into account that family entertainment (the true need) could be provided by a zoo, museum, or an amusement park. However, the owner should not consider a movie rental to be a direct competitor.

This section will require you to do a quick competitive analysis, so you understand what you're up against. Highlight at least five competitors, although there may be more. If so, you should narrow your scope. If there are only a few competitors, broaden your scope to include substitute offerings as well. [7] The threat of having fewer competitors is that they may control dedicated distribution channels, suppliers, or materials that are critical to success in that line of business.

2. Competitor Analysis

You need to know the competition's strengths and weaknesses.

Strengths

What is the competition best known for? Which aspects of your competitors' offerings are impossible for you to duplicate? These are things that your competition will leverage against you, and you must have something that will counter the scale in your favor.

A great (although common) example is Wal-Mart. Its strength is its distribution system. The competition would find it extremely difficult to duplicate what they have done, despite the attempts of most retailers.

---

7 Substitutes are offerings which satisfy your customer's need differently than yours. In fact, the offering is completely different! If you are selling chocolate bars, your product is competing with other chocolate bars. You might even consider any chocolate dessert or cookie to be in competition with your product. But, have you included lemon meringue pie? Or a second helping of the main dish? Or hot chocolate? Or a diet? Many of these alternative ways of fulfilling the need may not be included in your list of competitors and are considered substitutes.

Weaknesses

You can only capitalize on your competitors' weaknesses if you can identify them. What does your competition lack? What have they overlooked? What do current customers dislike about them? These are all aspects to consider in providing better value to your potential customers.

An example here could be a movie store. Large chains are excellent at keeping new releases in stock, but they rarely have the classic, older movies. This might be a market niche to exploit, and a way to outshine Rogers or Blockbuster (as long as the numbers make sense!).

Form 2 will help you perform a quick competitive analysis.

Form 2   Competitive Analysis

Competition	Major Strength	Major Weakness

3. Competitive Edge

Once you have identified and researched your competition, you can begin to understand how your offering is unique. Your offering must be different and better than the competition's.

Consider your offering:

- Is your offering different from what is currently available?
- Is it better than the competition's offerings?
- What competition are you up against?
- Is this an uphill battle that you can win?

- Is there a competitor who fulfills the need more completely than you could?
- If so, can you offer more value? This is your competitive edge.

For example, an ice cream store may make its ice cream with the highest quality ingredients and have the most flavors. But, if the customers want vanilla soft serve, this won't make a difference and they will continue to go to McDonald's.

Do not choose price as a factor. It's not all about your price; it is about the value that you provide for the price. So, if you only offer a book, but someone else offers a CD, book and online involvement pieces at the same price, then your offering has a problem. You either need to offer more or sell for less. The value has to be superior.

There are many different ways to develop a competitive edge. Even though your competitor is extremely strong, you can still have a market advantage. To be successful, you merely have to be stronger in one component that is important to the customer. For example, you could focus on:

- Ease of use
- Low-cost distribution network
- Knowledgeable sales staff
- Patented feature
- Customized solutions
- Tireless sales staff
- Fast delivery
- Brand name loyalty or trust
- Convenience
- Time saving
- Quirky advertising
- Personal relationship

If the customer values on-time delivery over low cost, you have created more value than the competition if you are on time more often than they. Being #1 for something that is important to the customer gives you a competitive edge! It is better to be the large fish in the small pool than a little fish in a large pool. Establish leadership for something.

K-Mart tried to emulate Wal-Mart's distribution system, to be the low-cost provider, but they were always #2 on the ladder. By contrast, Target sought to establish a positive brand image, thus differentiating itself. Target made itself special (and successful) by becoming the best in one area that the customer valued.

If the customer does not care about the component you have determined as your competitive edge, you will not be successful. Value will not have been created. Focus on something that is at the top of the minds of your target market. For example, you might have homemade ice cream made from real cream. However, if the target customer is more interested in the number of toppings or the type of cones you have available, this difference will not result in increased sales.

We cannot be everything to all people. The niche market is vital. By going after the niche customer who has very specific needs, we are no longer going directly against the competition. We are playing a new game that they may not have even heard of! Niche markets also create a clearer vision for employees.[8] That is your goal, and the entire operations and marketing strategy should support this.

If you cannot compete in one niche market, choose a new niche market where you meet the customer's needs more fully than the competition and therefore offer more value. Chapter Five explains how to select your niche market.

4. Competitor Retaliation

Once you launch, what is the likelihood that competitors will retaliate? 100%.

---

8 Vision is the guiding light of the organization. Having a vision in an organization gives the employee base the information they need to help direct each and every movement they make. For example, if the vision is to have the best customer service in the industry, then all the employees know that they have leeway to go the extra mile for a customer – no matter the cost. If the vision is to be the most creative company, different actions by the employee are implied.

"Be prepared for the competition to put up a fight"

You must realize that retaliation is bound to happen and you must enter the market with a plan to mitigate the damage or to keep ahead.

Often the differentiating point must be more than a product attribute, unless there is a patent to protect your advantage.[9] A patent is not a fail-safe solution, as there is the chance that the competition can tweak its design enough to enter the market. Further, a patent only lasts for twenty years. It is better to create something special or to combine many attributes, making it difficult for the competition to reproduce your offering.

An example of how to keep your offering unique is to take the situation of a coffee shop owner facing fierce competition. A new coffee shop would need something different to draw people from their preferred location. This could be some sort of entertainment, free samples, a wider variety of food options, or a more comfortable atmosphere. Even these are fairly standard variations. The best thing is to have something valued by customers, different and difficult to copy. If the owner were a master baker, she could decide to make one-of-a-kind pies each day. This might be something more difficult to copy, as large coffee chains have standardized product offerings, and are less able to adapt. Of

---

9 A patent is expensive and difficult to get. Not every product or service can be patented. Patents are further discussed in the next chapter.

course, this is only important if the local clientele likes pies and thinks that this type of product variety is important.

Time Tip: *This section of "Your Idea" takes the longest, as you might have to do some additional research to find and analyze your competition. If these requirements are already known, either because you have experience in the industry or the competition is well-known, the extra time isn't necessary.*

Quick & Easy Summary: Differentiation

- The number of competitors that you face depends on the scope that you've selected to be your industry.

- A competitive analysis identifies the competition's strengths and weaknesses to find a gap where you can create a competitive edge.

- A competitive edge must differentiate your offering from the competition's offering and be important to the customer to be effective.

- Expect the competition to retaliate. You would!

Your Idea Test

Is there a genuine need and does your product meet that need better than the available alternatives?

If not, there are still things to consider:

1. Is Your Target Market Just Unaware That They Have a Need?

The most difficult thing for a company to communicate to a customer is the awareness of a need. The phenomenon identified by Geoffrey Moore, known as "Crossing the Chasm," shows that it is extremely difficult to educate the general public about a specific need that they might have (especially for technology offerings). It took the personal computer decades to cross the chasm, CDs years, and some concepts never reach the mainstream. This is the hardest thing to convince a customer of, so if there is no obvious need to the customer, your idea most likely will fail. On the flip side, those entrepreneurs who did cross the chasm have re-invented what was needed.

Your message for an offering with an unrealized need would have to focus on explaining to the target market that the need exists. This type of business idea has higher risk. It is still possible, just significantly less so!

2. Are You Providing Value to Your Customers?

A customer's willingness-to-pay is fundamental. If the customer does not perceive value – above and beyond the costs to create the offering – there is no willingness-to-pay.

Price and cost are the two components of value. What are other things you could do to add value above and beyond your basic inputs? Are there costs that can be taken out?

3. Can Your Offering Fulfill the Need Better Than the Alternative?

Have you fully identified the customer's needs? Are there additional gaps in your offering that the competition is taking advantage of, or could take advantage of in the future? Are there additional services or complementary products that you could add to the offering to fill those gaps?

If this test proves that your idea might not fly... STOP!

If this test proves that it might be easier than you thought possible... GO! GO! GO!

Quick & Easy Summary: Your Idea

- To start, you need a product/service concept which includes a specific business model.

- All great ideas start with a need and end in an offering.

- An offering should be a mix of both products and services, which add value to the customer.

- Your offering must be different from your competitors' and difficult to duplicate in order to be successful.

CHAPTER THREE:
THE NUMBERS

The Second Test Stage

So, you've passed the first test stage in the Idea Tester framework. Congratulations. We'll now move on to the second stage of testing. Recall from Table A that this stage is given a 35% weighting in the overall testing framework. As a reminder of how much time to commit to each section of this stage, part of Table A has been replicated below.

Table E   The Numbers Framework

Test Stage Weighting	*Stage Sections*	*Suggested Time Commitment*
The Numbers (35%)	Cost of Being in Business	50%
	Profit Margin	30%
	Break-Even Point	10%
	Test	10%
	Total	100%

The goal of this section is to determine the **idea's** financial feasibility.

Most of us are in business to make money, so we don't want to move to the next test until we know that we stand a very good chance of making money. You are taking a risk and investing a lot of time in the idea, so it is likely that you are hoping for some sort of financial reward.

So the real question is, When are we making money? In its simplest form, profit is made the moment that all of your costs have been covered. This profit is what will belong to the entrepreneur. If starting a business is all about making money, then it is important to know how many sales need to be made before the money starts rolling in!

How does one determine whether he or she is going to make money? The questions that need to be posed are the following:

1. How much will it cost to start the business? (cost)

2. How much money will be made on each sale? (margin)

3. How much must be sold in order to pay off the initial investment? (break-even sales goals)

The key is to understand your costs, your margin, and the sales goals required to make profits. These components will determine whether the **idea** is profitable.

If the idea cannot make money, there is no point moving it forward. There are a few challenges to consider in determining the idea's profitability:

1. In your first year, you may incur different expenses than in future years. You might expect to lose money in the first few years, depending on how high your initial investment is. This can be taken into account by doing an analysis for a two-year period or doing an analysis separately for each year of operation. Adjust the model to work for you.

   For a simple business model, it is best to do an analysis for the first year. Since a business idea changes often, it is unlikely your profits will come from exactly where you think they will in future years.

2. There are so many costs that it could take a long time to do the background work necessary for the numbers to be

accurate. Even then, things change and there will be hidden or unforeseen costs. This can be overcome by focusing on your main cost drivers. Use estimates for smaller costs, but ensure that you research any cost that may have a large impact on the company's financial feasibility.

For example, if your idea is to open a retail store, then the cost of labour, the cost of products to be sold, and the store rent will be your largest costs. You should spend more time investigating these, rather than the cost of registering your business or developing business cards.

Time Tip: Most numbers in this chapter require some research in advance. Always keep in mind that the time you spend has a cost – you could be spending it in moving your idea forward. Time is precious. Understand that there is a trade-off to having more information to make better decisions and the time it takes to gather this information. Investigate information around key cost drivers, but estimate the others.

Cost of Being in Business (Fixed Costs)

What does it take to move your idea forward? What are the physical items that are required in order for you to say that you have your own business? By thinking in these terms, as opposed to expanding upon your initial concept, you are able to focus on first steps and begin acting.

It also determines something very important – can you **afford** it? If you don't have the money necessary to start up your business idea (even after including your access to loans or other funding), then there isn't any point wasting time thinking about this idea. Wait for the next one. Move on.

How does one determine if the idea is affordable? Simple. If you were going to start this business tomorrow, what would you need? To figure out how much money is required, you need to identify the basic costs that you will face each month (at least until you actually begin making money) and the necessary start-up costs, in order to create a reasonable infrastructure to be in business. These are called fixed costs.

Fixed costs are those incurred by your business even if you don't sell a single service or product. These costs include professional advice, initial business registration, legal and accounting fees, marketing costs, office rent and furniture, salaries, equipment, office supplies, utilities, and a slush fund. This list may not be exhaustive for the business you intend to create. The key to identifying these costs is, **they are not dependent on sales volume**. You have to pay these costs just to be in business.

Fixed costs add risk to a business. The higher the fixed costs your business has, the more sales you have to make to pay off this initial investment. For start-up businesses, every dollar saved in fixed costs, increases the probability that the idea will fly. The remainder of this chapter not only outlines the components of your fixed costs in order to tabulate them, but also suggests how you could look at cutting these costs.

You should limit this planning to your first year in business, but you can use this framework for subsequent years. Once your company begins growing, the fixed costs may increase, as most businesses are not infinitely scalable.[10] For instance, you might need to hire new sales staff or customer service representatives to handle the sales volume. This results in higher rent, since you now need more office space. The fixed costs you should focus on are the initial costs related to initial volume; you will only expand your business once it has proven to be extremely successful. On the flip side, there are some business costs which will never recur, such as business registration. So, when planning for subsequent years, your fixed costs will change.

Note that large investments in your company have been excluded from fixed costs! We are determining how much cash you need on hand to be able to establish your business, making you responsible only for principle and interest to pay for these large investments. It is assumed that you have already been given the financing for the business. We are focused on **cash outflows**.

Awareness of your cash outflows allows you to develop a plan to deal with them. For example, if a coffee shop owner has only a little bit of money to start up, he or she may mitigate costs by leasing the building rather than buying, by offering a limited number of products rather than a complete range, by starting with a sole-proprietorship rather than incorporating, or by utilizing his or her network for legal, accounting, and marketing help rather than hiring professionals.

The possible initial start-up expenses that you might be facing in order to be in business are outlined in Form 3. These are not exhaustive for all businesses, and some of them may not be applicable to your business, but it will give you a good starting framework.

---

10 Being scalable means having the ability to serve an exponential number of customers without spending more money on fixed costs. An example would be Facebook. As soon as the basic programming was completed, an infinite number of people could be served without spending additional money as a company. AND this happened over a very short period of time.

Form 3   Cost of Being in Business

Business Cost	Per Month	Per Year
Business Registration		
Legal / Accounting Fees		
Marketing: Graphics / Business Cards / Website / Advertising / Signs		
Office: Rent / Equipment / Furniture/ Computer / Printer / Supplies		
Warehouse: Rent / Equipment		
Factory: Rent		
Factory: Equipment		
Salaries		
Telephone / Internet		
Insurance		
Interest		
Slush Fund (Other)		
Total Cost of Being in Business		

Business Registration

The good thing is that you only have to face this cost once! The cost here can vary from a few hundred dollars to a few thousand dollars. Just like estimating any expense, it is important to be realistic, and if in doubt, pick the higher number. Developing your own sole-proprietorship is the cheapest route for a start-up business, especially if you choose your own name for the company. This avoids the added expense of a business name search. However, there are liability implications further down the line, which may make a corporation more attractive. Although incorporating may be more expensive up front, it will protect you from this liability. Also, there are costs in registering trademarks for your business name, tagline, and logo.

Helpful Links: Business Ownership

http://www.smallbusinessbc.ca/bizstart-prop.php

http://investincanada.gc.ca/eng/establish-a-business/business-structure-select.aspx

---

Legal Fees

These could be as simple as having someone help you with developing customer contracts, registering your business, or creating the partnership agreement. Although not something we like to consider, it is always important to have good legal counsel close at hand. Having legal counsel up front, someone who understands your business, will help you in the long-run.

How could you look at reducing these costs?

Ever thought about bartering? This is a method that is far more common than most people realize, especially for a start-up company, which is usually cash poor. Consider negotiating within your network to exchange your product/service for something you want. This could apply to legal, accounting, marketing, or business strategy services. Be creative!

Accounting Fees

With the introduction of accounting software, there are alternatives! However, many accounting students (and even accounting firms) can set up your books or do periodic reviews for a reasonable fee.

Marketing

So much falls under marketing!

Some types of marketing are free, including word-of-mouth advertising, newspaper articles and speaking engagements. The marketing of your business must be professional and consistent. At minimum, you require the skills of a graphic designer to create your basic marketing pieces. Good graphic designers are able to create a unique logo and may help you with your business name. Great graphic designers often are able to create websites, brochures, newsletters, photographs, and much more. They also have a great network of suppliers able to produce business cards and signage very quickly. It is a good idea to get someone on your side in this industry because it saves time reiterating what you're looking for. Once you are sure that they understand your business and the general look-and-feel you want, you will be able to give them free license to be creative.[11] You will be pleasantly surprised by the results.

Don't forget that you'll be doing a lot of networking during this time, and these events cost money to attend. Networking costs can be mitigated by going to community events, doing volunteer work, or acting as the keynote speaker at events. However, many events will take both your time and your money, so make sure that you choose strategically the ones in which you wish to take part.

Office

Do you need an office? Is this necessary?

You are already living somewhere, and take into consideration that office expenses are quite prohibitive. The fewer costs that

---

11 Look-and-feel is exactly what it indicates. This is how your marketing and communication tools are perceived by your customer audience and how this feeling is then widened to represent the rest of the company. Examples of good words to put in a creative brief to assist graphic designers in understanding your look-and-feel: fresh, young, professional, happy, creative, classic, funky, etc.

your new company incurs, the fewer sales are required to pay back this money. Without additional expenses, your company has a better chance of success. Try to purchase things as you **need** them rather than when you **want** them.

There are, however, very practical reasons for having an office:

- You have employees, so you need to offer a location for them. Alternatively, you have elected to supervise them, which requires them to be on site.

- Part of marketing is to offer an image of professionalism and stability and an office provides this.

- You need a physical location for clients and employees to meet face-to-face.

There are many services available which will allow your business to have a physical presence without having large fixed overhead costs. One option is to work with the local Board of Trade and use its facilities. Get in contact with a business realtor who may have contacts wishing to share space at a reduced cost. Other considerations include businesses that rent part-time physical space, P.O. boxes and answering services that give the impression you have an office.

If you do need an office, make sure that you incorporate all the costs that come with it. The office setup comes with property taxes, furniture, computers, utilities, rent and maintenance. You should also include commuting time.

"Do you need an office?"

Factory

Do you need this? It is a huge fixed cost!

In fact, there are major advantages to **not** having your own factory in addition to the major cost savings: (a) You have fewer employees (further reducing your fixed costs); (b) You can focus on other parts of your business which might add more value to the customer.

There are good reasons to have your own factory. Some industries cannot be outsourced. The requirements of your product may be so strict that no one else produces it. The product/service quality may be so important that you require control over the manufacturing process. There may be some R&D that needs to be protected by keeping the process as company information.

Some options to reduce the requirement for a factory **or** eliminate the need for a factory:

- Buy pre-assembled components and only do final assembly, reducing the amount of space necessary.

- Buy the final product from a company and act solely as the distributor without doing any manufacturing.

Ensure that your decision to own a factory is tied to your business strategy and that the initial start-up costs are justified. Most importantly, make sure that these additional costs are not the burden that prevents your business from being successful.

Warehouse

This is another large fixed cost. It is becoming more common for companies to develop their distribution networks with more regional distribution centres to satisfy customer requests quickly and mitigate the rising cost of fuel.

Advantages of **not** having your own warehouses include fewer employees to manage, less restriction to distribution regions, and the ability to use up-to-date systems.

There are still reasons why it might be important for a company to have its own warehouses: warehouses might be required for returns or recycling (reverse logistics), for on-time customer delivery, or for after-sales service. A company may have its own warehouses because it believes that it can keep the costs of the above lower than an outside provider could.

Some options which reduce the need for a warehouse:

- Sell the product or service directly to the customer from the factory.

- Sell the idea to a broker, buying agent, or a distributor. This allows you to act as the customer rather than the seller. This puts the onus on someone else and may require you only to buy products and ship to them as required. You then don't need to rent a warehouse, and your partner incurs more of the risk.

Be sure that your decision to own a warehouse is tied to your business strategy. Determine that the initial start-up costs being poured out make sense and are not the extra load that prevents your business from being successful.

Patents, Copyrights & Trademarks

These are costs that will protect your intellectual property for an extended period of time. Although none of them are required for starting up a new business, they are good to have in order to protect your idea in the future. If your business becomes as successful as you'd like it to be, you'll want to ensure that you're not changing your business logo, name, or company information in the future because another company is mimicking them. Initial marketing costs and effort would then be wasted.

Patents are an excellent way to have an edge over the competition, as this gives your idea protection for twenty years. However, patents are costly and if the competition comes up with an idea that is even slightly different, there is no protection. In fact, in many cases, the best protection is to keep your "secret" safe.

Coca-Cola has a secret recipe which has never been patented. The reason? A patent only lasts for twenty years and requires that you detail your product or idea. Coca-Cola has been able to protect its recipe much better and for much longer without a patent.

In addition, getting a patent can be difficult, as three requirements must be met. A product or service can be patented if it is:

1. Useful
2. Novel
3. Non-obvious

The helpful links section provides resources in order to further help you in protecting your intellectual property.

Helpful Links: Intellectual Property

http://en.wikipedia.org/wiki/Intellectual_property

Patents:

www.cipo.ic.gc.ca/patents
http://www.ic.gc.ca/eic/site/cipointernet-internetopic.nsf/eng/wr
00141.html

Copyright:

http://www.cipo.ic.gc.ca/eic/site/cipointernet-internetopic.nsf/eng/
h_wr00003.html?OpenDocument
http://www.cb-cda.gc.ca/info/act-e.html
http://www.copyright.gov/

Trademarks:

https://strategis.ic.gc.ca/sc_mrksv/cipo/trademark-filing/application
/engdoc/index_owner_e.html
http://www.ic.gc.ca/app/opic-cipo/trdmrks/srch/tmSrch.do?lang=eng

Research & Development

Unlike patents, this up-front cost is required. In fact, without a prototype, you will not be funded by anyone, since you don't have anything to sell. It is recommended that you have the skills to perform your own R&D, in order to minimize these costs and ensure the integrity of the research. For most hi-tech industries, this will be the largest start-up cost.

Salaries

I might sound like a broken record, but salaries might also be postponed at the beginning of a business – until the hiring of additional staff can be justified by sales volumes. If you don't have the skills or the time to perform what is required for the business, then salaries are inevitable. For example, if you are opening a hair salon, you need to know how to cut hair, or you need to hire someone who does. If you are launching a restaurant with long hours, then this time commitment is required either by you or your staff.

Your salary should **not** be included in this section. We are going to keep that separate, in order to determine if the business is feasible versus whether the business will meet **your** expectations.

Telephone & Internet

These are self-explanatory and necessary in today's connected environment.

Insurance

Insurance is also necessary for most businesses. Depending on what industry your business is in, some forms of insurance may be required while others are recommended. Speak to an insurance agent to better understand the requirements in your field. Better yet, speak to two of them for comparison.

Interest

There is a high likelihood that you will need to use credit cards, borrow from family/friends or incur alternative debt to start up the business. If these relationships aren't maintained, or if payments are missed, there will be no business. It is imperative to keep this expense top of mind.

Slush Fund (Other)

Although it is safer to overestimate all expenses, it is also smart to prepare for "surprise" expenses. You cannot account for everything that will happen during your start up. It would be prudent to protect your business, planning for unanticipated expenses by having additional money on-hand as a buffer.

Examples of unforeseen increases in cost are the price of utilities or advertising. Fuel prices can fluctuate greatly over a given year. For this example, any time anything in a business is transported, unanticipated costs are incurred.

Note: High Capital Investments

High fixed costs should be handled in this section by accounting for the necessary interest payments and the specified amount of principle that is expected to be paid off. If your company is working toward the purchase of expensive fixed assets through venture capitalist funding, then those fixed assets are not included here. The amount of money necessary to get to the point of venture capitalist funding is important.

Total Cost of Being in Business

This number is the end result – your fixed costs required to be in business.

Quick & Easy Summary: Cost of Being in Business

- The cost of being in business is the total of all fixed costs involved in your business.

- Fixed costs are any costs that your business incurs regardless of sales. You could have zero sales and these costs would still exist.

- Fixed costs are dramatically different for each company, depending on your offering and your business model. You need to customize this analysis for your business idea.

Profit Margin

Profit: the real reason we are in business.

Let me qualify that statement. There are some individuals not driven by profit. It may be a hobby; they may believe in the offering's altruistic value; it's a side gig; or they are just able to pay the bills. Primarily, however, businesses are run to achieve a profit.

Even a not-for-profit organization needs to understand its profit margin, since its main objective is to stay in business and to serve the company's mission. It can't do this without meeting its fixed costs, so there must be margin somewhere.

So, let's reiterate. Profit: the real reason we are in business.

Everything I Learned About Profit Margin, I Learned in China

I learned a life lesson in profit margin during my four-month stint in China. Often, I left a store feeling that I was getting the best of a bargaining session, or that there was little point in the merchant being in business with such low prices.

But there is a **new** Chinese proverb: "Nobody is losing money in China."

The Chinese merchants understand margin better than anyone… anywhere. If a store owner in China is negotiating with you, his or her focus is on margin. Here is an example of the mentality that I was faced with, and still marvel at today.

Stage 1: You are negotiating for a purse and have brought it from a starting price of $100 down to $20. The merchant will appear upset that the price has dropped so much. She will tell you that she is making "no money," in this transaction. However, she knows that her fixed costs are met at $5 per purse, and therefore, her margin is actually $15. Since she is not satisfied with that margin, the negotiations will continue, even though you were happy with one purse at $20…

Stage 2: The storekeeper asks how many purses you wish to purchase. You say, "One." But she finds out that you have two sisters-in-law back home, so you receive a price of $60 for three purses. The storekeeper is now looking at a margin of $45 (cost is $5 x 3 = $15) if you accept. If you don't, negotiations will continue. She will work hard to increase her margin beyond the original $15…

Stage 3: The seller keeps the bargaining going, with the price for three purses dropping to $50. She realizes that margin is king and that means anything above cost. A larger quantity sale, even when discounted, means that her margin rises to $35 from the initial $15 ($50 price subtract $15 cost). This bargaining game will continue until the storekeeper's margin rises or the customer refuses to negotiate.

How does this concept apply to your business?

"How much money am I making?"

You need to understand how much you can sell your offering for (your price) versus how much it will cost you to deliver (your variable cost). The difference is your profit per sale (your **margin**).

Margin can be counted in many different ways. In the end you are either making money or not, but margin can be tabulated for:

- Single offerings (single transactions)
- Groups of offerings (package deals)
- Fixed amounts of time (contracts)

Let's get some examples:

- Single offering – one purse which results in a $20 margin
- Group of offerings – three purses which result in a $35 margin.
- Fixed amount of time – one customer's lifetime value is thirty purses for a $350 margin

Determining One Sale

So, before understanding your offering's price, costs and margin, we have to decide how to measure "One Sale" to make the rest of the model consistent. The end result will be the ability to figure out how many One Sales it will take to pay off your cost of being in business and to start making money.

You need to determine what is considered a One Sale for your business. There is sometimes a choice to be made: a customer who purchases an offering only once a year can be counted on a fixed amount of time basis, or on a single offering basis. A hair dresser could measure the One Sale by a fixed amount of time (as usually customers are loyal and require 8 haircuts a year) or by the number of haircuts performed. The key is to be consistent. Once you decide how to measure One Sale, stick to it.

If you still don't know how best to measure One Sale, answer the questions below to help you decide.

- **Does your customer sign a yearly contract?**
  If yes, One Sale is a fixed amount of time, which can be measured by the number of customers. One of the best examples is a cell phone plan, in which a customer signs a one- to three-year contract. The cell phone companies should be measuring the lifetime value of each customer.

- **Can your customer order any number of products/services at one time?**
  If yes, One Sale is a single offering, which can be measured by the number of units sold. The example here would be any consumer packaged goods product, including ketchup, waffles, or sausages. Each one is purchased independently and the margin is counted per product.

- **Does a customer typically order accessories or add-ons at one time?**
  If yes, One Sale is a group of offerings, which can be measured by the number of packages sold. An example might be a game

system, which is purchased with an average number of games to accompany it.

Often a company sells more than one product or service. For simplicity, use the average price and average cost for all the products and services which your company will be selling.

Unfortunately, estimating costs often involves making a lot of assumptions. There is a trade-off between the time and money required to gather information and the benefit that can be realized from this research. It is important to find a happy medium.

For example, if a florist underestimates the cost of transporting flowers by 15%, that is a larger mistake than underestimating the price of receipt paper by 50%. The flower transportation cost estimate was off by a smaller percentage, but the overall cost implications to the company are much larger than the trivial cost of receipt paper. I recommend in the idea testing stage researching all of your largest costs; making an error by just a bit on these costs could significantly impact your numbers. Smaller costs are simply not worth the time to investigate at this early stage. As in the case of estimating the costs of being in business, when in doubt, estimate on the high side.

With your One Sale in mind, let's figure out your offering's price, cost, and margin for each One Sale.

Price per One Sale

Price must be lower than the total value you are providing to a customer. The complete product and service offering that you are providing must be "worth it" to purchase. When creating price points, ensure that the product is "worth" that amount.

Think about whether you want to charge a price that is low, medium, or high. This is important, as by charging lower versus higher prices, you are targeting a different customer. There is a trade-off.

- Lower prices mean that you will attract more customers, but you will make less money per One Sale.

- Higher prices mean a lower customer volume, but a higher margin contribution.

An earring wholesaler may charge a very low price per pair of earrings to retailers, but they must sell millions of pairs of earrings to remain profitable at this lower price. An earring retailer who charges a higher price may only sell a few thousand pairs of earrings. If a retailer has a low enough price, other retailers might buy directly from them. However, with this lower price (and lower margin), they would have to sell a larger quantity to remain profitable. Another example is small corner stores buying chocolate bars and bottled water for resale from Costco.

Cost per One Sale (Variable Costs)

Costs per One Sale are direct costs that are incurred due to an incremental sale. Unlike fixed costs, if sales are not increasing, neither will these costs. Costs per One Sale are called variable costs and can include:

- **Materials**
  These are the cost of the inputs or physical materials that go into the offering. Materials can vary from raw materials, components, accessories, or the cost of the product at wholesale value. Sometimes an offering has more than one input cost.

- **Direct Labour**
  These costs include the physical labour which is used to make, sell, or distribute a product. Make sure that you do **not** count your labour cost twice, as salaries were included in the cost of being in business. Labour which is paid for on a per unit basis is easy to calculate here. Any salary work, where the costs remain static regardless of sales volume, should be considered a fixed cost rather than a variable cost.

- **Shipping**

  Shipping costs can include any pick-and-pack work, storage, shipping, etc. Basically, shipping costs include any cost that is a direct result of delivering the offering.[12]

- **Sales**

  Direct sales costs include commissions or sales tools.

It should also be noted that the cost of an offering may decrease over time, due to the learning curve or economies of scale.[13,14] However, using future projected numbers rather than real ones increases the risk of not meeting your expectations. Always be as realistic as possible. Use Form 4 to calculate your cost per One Sale.

Form 4   Cost per One Sale

Cost Description	Amount
Materials	
Direct Labour	
Shipping	
Sales	
Total Costs	

---

12 Pick-and-pack is a unique service offered by most commercial warehouses, where the company will perform all order taking, shipping instructions, and packaging of your product for direct delivery to your customers. This is handy for a large product mix or for companies with limited space. It is also a great solution if you want to start up a business without incurring your own warehousing fixed costs.

13 A learning curve occurs when the direct labour cost per unit decreases as employees perform duties faster through repetition or training. This happens in almost any process. Just as you can get better at biking, swimming or hockey, an employee can get better at any process in your business. The adage, Practice makes perfect, is true in this case.

14 Economies of scale occur when the direct overhead cost per unit decreases as more products are being made, without changing the fixed costs. For example, your factory requires ten large boxes of fabric for production. You might consider reducing the associated shipping costs by purchasing twenty large boxes instead. Purchasing twenty boxes does not double the shipping cost; rather, the shipping cost would likely increase by only 50%. If you purchase twenty boxes, you pay lower shipping costs per box than if you only purchase ten.

Margin per One Sale

Margin per One Sale is easily calculated by subtracting the total cost per One Sale from the price per One Sale. Now you have identified how much money you are able to make on each One Sale completed. Since the main objective of most companies is to make a profit, this number is crucial and will be used throughout the remainder of the book. Use Form 5 to calculate your margin per One Sale.

Form 5   Margin per One Sale

Description	Amount
Price per One Sale	
- Cost per One Sale	
= Margin per One Sale	

Your cost per One Sale may be **higher** than your price per One Sale, meaning your business idea is not able to provide enough value to customers to give you a profit. If this is the case, then your idea is not feasible. You need either to change the offering design (in order to charge a higher price), or to lower your costs by removing non-value adding pieces.

Consider the following situation. A towel distributor wishes to sell directly to customers using home delivery. However, the customer is unwilling to pay the extra $5 delivery charge and continues to go to a local retailer. There is not enough value for the customer to buy directly. The customer may be willing to pay an extra $1 for home delivery, but if the towel distributor cannot reduce his operating costs to meet this $1 price point, the idea is not feasible. Other options here would be to add more value to the towel. A special type of fabric only found through this distribution channel could be offered. The towel distributor could sell only to hotels, for whom the delivery fee per towel would be lower and for whom the cost of picking up a few hundred towels at a retail store is too high.

Using the towel distributor example, you can see that to create margin, you must either increase the value of your offering, allowing you to increase the price, or eliminate features of your offering that do not add customer value, allowing you to reduce your cost.

Margin Percentage

Margin is often calculated as a percentage of price. This is calculated as follows.

% Margin = Margin per One Sale / Price per One Sale

What is an ideal percentage? This differs by industry and business model.

Industry

Industry players either have strength or don't. If your business is in an industry with very strong players (either your suppliers, customers, service providers, or your direct competitors), your offering will probably have a lower margin. If you are the strong player in the industry, your offering will probably have a higher margin. If a new product is just entering an industry's market, it is in the introductory stage with fewer competitors, meaning that margins are higher.

Business Model

If you utilize the Internet for business, or have few fixed costs, you can get away with a slim margin. However, if you have a physical location, or have high fixed costs, normally you will need a higher margin to help cover these costs. If the business model has many distributors or marketing expenses, the margins have to be high enough to facilitate proper distribution and to compensate all the players.

It is impossible to say whether a margin percentage is ideal or not without understanding both the industry and the business model.

Quick & Easy Summary: Profit Margin

- Determine what you classify as One Sale for your offering.

- Choose a price where your cost of inputs is lower than the value you can provide.

- Costs per One Sale are costs which increase as more sales are made. These are not part of the cost of being in business (fixed costs), which should not be repeated here (especially salaries).

- Margin is the difference between the price of the offering and the cost of the inputs to deliver the offering.

Break-Even Point

The book so far has developed building blocks to prepare your business idea for the ultimate test – the break-even analysis. In its simplest form, the break-even point is:

How many One Sales do you need to pay off **all** of your costs of being in business?

A pleasant thought – anything over this number of One Sales will result in margin that will make its way into your pocket… Your profit!

The formula is simple.

Break-Even One Sales =
Cost of Being in Business / Margin per One Sale

This tool is powerful. If you know how many One Sales you require in order to make money, you are able to calculate your minimum sales on an annual, a monthly, weekly, and/or daily basis.

"This tool is powerful!"

Take all of the previous data and fill in Form 6.

Form 6   Break-Even

Description	How to Get this Number	Your Numbers
Total Cost of Being in Business	Chapter Three – Cost of Being in Business	
Price per One Sale	Chapter Three – Profit Margin	
Total Cost per One Sale	Chapter Three – Profit Margin	
Margin per One Sale	Chapter Three – Profit Margin	
Break-Even Yearly Target	Total Cost of Being in Business / Profit Margin	
Break-Even Monthly Target	Break-Even Yearly Target / 12	
Break-Even Weekly Target*	Break-Even Yearly Target / 50	
Break-Even Daily Target**	Break-Even Yearly Target / 250	

*based on 50 weeks of the year

**based on 250 days of the year

Time Tip: *All of these calculations are automatically provided to you when using the questionnaire at www.makeitfly.ca. In addition, you will be informed of where your business stands versus the industry average.*

The entrepreneur is empowered by understanding how much has to be sold within a specified time period. Your marketing plan should be developed to meet to these targets.

If you only need one customer per week in order to pay off the start-up costs of your business, marketing campaigns can be developed to target a niche market instead of over-investing in broad marketing techniques. For example, a computer programmer charges $10,000 for annual licensing fees, and the initial development cost of the business is $60,000 (including the salary of the programmer and the cost of a new computer).

Break-Even Units = $60,000 / $10,000
= 6 license agreements / year

With these costs of being in business and margin per One Sale, the programmer knows:

- six licensing agreements need to be sold every year
- one licensing agreement needs to be sold every two months

Thinking in this light has made the idea seem feasible. With this knowledge, she doesn't have to develop a program suited to every business. She can make her offering extremely niche-targeted, since she doesn't need a ton of customers. She has minimized her costs and maximized her margin.

The reverse is also true. If you discover that you need a huge number of sales per day in order to cover your business costs, you need to reconsider whether this is feasible and begin thinking about the marketing implications. If you need 50% of your target market to buy the product to break even, the business idea is not feasible.

Here is the reverse example. A coffee shop is looking at a location that costs $100,000 per year in rent. Since the owners want the shop to be open 250 days a year, salaries will amount to another $100,000. The shop will need $50,000 in renovations to open. The coffee shop's start-up costs total $250,000. However, the shop is making a margin at only $1 per cup of coffee and $1 per baked good.

Break-Even Units = $250,000 / $1 = 250,000 sales / year

With these start-up costs and margin, the owners know:

- 250,000 cups of coffee or baked goods need to be sold every year

- 1,000 cups of coffee or baked goods need to be sold each day

Thinking this way has made these entrepreneurs face some harsh realities. What strategies can be used to draw in the one thousand customers per day? Do these customers come all at once? Are there seasonal fluctuations? These numbers will highlight other details as possible issues (such as having enough seating for one thousand customers), making the business idea much more difficult to execute, and perhaps not feasible.

Every business is different and can use this information in different ways. Assess the numbers on which your company needs to focus.

Yearly Target

All companies need to pay attention to their annual targets. If a company is not meeting the daily, weekly, or monthly targets, there is an excellent chance that the annual targets won't be met either.

Some business ideas may **only** use the yearly target. These businesses' offerings are higher cost and may only require one or two sales per year to stay afloat. Usually in these cases, the sales processes, payment period and implementation of the service require much time. It would not make sense to judge a company's success on a daily basis. But, it will be empowered by the yearly target.

An example may be that of a consulting practice. Often, offerings are longer contracts of between six and twelve months, requiring a lot of up-front legwork. The consultant must scope out the project, build a relationship, and close the sale. If a consulting practice requires two contracts per year to break even, it is able to identify a problem at six months through the year when the consultant sees that there isn't even one customer coming on board. The consultant knows at that point that he needs to get moving! This type of company does not need to pay attention to the monthly, weekly, or daily targets. The yearly targets suffice.

Monthly & Weekly Targets

Monthly and weekly targets are best for offerings with peaks and valleys in demand. There might be a week within a month where there is little business, but then many customers show up the next week. The monthly volumes, however, aren't affected. Trucking companies may use monthly targets, as they are unsure how long different routes might take their drivers, and they are not sure when their customers will need their services. However, they know that they have to pay their drivers each month and that there is a certain amount of freight to be moved during a typical month.

Similarly, there might be a day within a given week where there is no business or perhaps 50% of the business is done on Saturdays. This might be true for a reception hall, where most weddings, company parties, and other social events are booked on the weekend. A daily or yearly target is not as important to this type of company as a weekly target.

Seasonality can be handled by paying attention to your yearly targets and skewing sales targets for the peak months. If you know how much needs to be sold per year, but 60% of the customer traffic is going to be between September and December, you can adjust your monthly targets accordingly. This specific scenario might be common for retail stores or an ice cream truck.

Daily Targets

This target is primarily used by companies with even traffic flows. The best examples would be a coffee shop or a hair salon. Knowing how many cups of coffee or how many haircuts a day must be sold allows the company to understand whether or not these numbers are realistic.

Once you know your daily targets, you can determine if these sales targets are realistic. Do that many people even *walk by* your business? Do you have a way of reaching that many people? Of course, this target could be broken down by the hour as well.

Other Uses

Not only does this break-even tool enable you to assess your idea, but it also allows you to:

- Prevent yourself from investing more money into the business if your idea is not turning out to be as successful as you had hoped. This minimizes your potential losses, as you begin to implement your idea.

- Monitor whether something has to change in the business model or whether you need to actually consider closing up shop (literally).

- Analyze your selected price point. You created a price point that is below the customer value that you provide, while making a reasonable margin. By using break-even targets, you are able to see the trade-off between your price and the required marketing initiatives to support them. If the price is higher, you do not have to sell as many products to pay off the start-up costs. But, consider how many customers can afford this higher price point. As you can see, this model will tie into your future marketing and operation strategies; you will have to deliver additional value to justify a higher price point. Conversely, at the lower price, is it possible to make the number of sales necessary to cover your costs?

- Perform a risk assessment. Break-even targets can be used to determine how much money your business might lose if you are 25% off in projecting your sales. How much money can your business make if you sell 10% more than expected? The break-even tool is powerful.

Innovation Myth: *Entrepreneurs are huge risk seekers. Successful entrepreneurs are not necessarily risk-adverse, but the difference is that they are willing to take calculated risks. They may have a vision that is unparalleled, but they do their market research and minimize their costs when it is prudent. They only take a perceived risk after weighing the options strategically.*

Quick & Easy Summary: Break-Even Point

- The break-even point is the number of One Sales it takes to pay off the cost of being in business (fixed costs).

- A marketing plan should be developed with these numbers in mind.

- Yearly, monthly, weekly, daily, and/or hourly sales targets should be chosen based on your business model, since they are helpful.

- Break-even targets help with day-to-day business monitoring and risk analysis.

Numbers Test

Will this idea make enough money to cover all of the costs involved in being in business?

If not, there are still things to consider:

1. Are all of these costs necessary up front?

Are there cheaper alternatives? In the Cost of Being in Business section, there are tips on how to reduce your start-up costs. There are businesses out there that provide almost anything with enticing payment options. There are also businesses that offer what you think you need to buy with short-term options. There are bartering alternatives for various services. There is also the option of considering a completely different, less expensive business model for the product.

Could this business be launched in stages? Does everything have to be done right now? The start-up costs should only include the bare minimum that is required to be "in business". They do not have to reflect your end vision. For many entrepreneurs, the minimum requirement is being able to secure their first sale out of their home office, garage, or parents' home. It can vary!

How long before these costs have to paid? Don't lose track of the fact that you are analyzing this idea for you. If you believe that it will take a few years before you can pay off your initial start-up costs and if you have the cash to sustain this, it may be reasonable to wait for a profit.

2. Do you have the financial resources or access to resources in order to get your first sale?

We looked at your costs as the amount required to be in business. If you have five potential customers already lined up, then you might as well be in business today. You can even factor in your profits from these sales to help pay for your start-up costs.

3. Can you adjust the price?

The key factor in the Idea Test is being realistic. Is your price point and required volume completely out of the park? Or is it realistic enough to develop a strategy to support this goal? If the answer isn't obvious, you should consider testing both price points and supporting business models until one emerges as the clear winner.

4. Are your variable costs prohibitive?

Can you reduce your offering's packaging or materials costs? Consider doing some of the packaging or assembly yourself or hire some local students. There is the side benefit that this type of employee is extremely eager, with tons of innovative ideas that can benefit your business.

Shipping costs can be reduced by shipping in larger quantities. This could be an option for your customers if you ship business-to-business.

Direct labour cost can be reduced through training or the proper incentive plan. This cost can also be reduced by hiring full-time employees; you then have to ensure that you have enough sales volume to justify this.

Direct sales costs can be reduced by training sales staff, tracking marketing techniques to learn what works best, or being more creative in your marketing. One way to reduce the sales cycle is to focus on referrals rather than cold calls.

If this test proves that your idea might not fly... STOP!

If this test proves that it might be easier than you thought possible... GO! GO! GO!

Quick & Easy Summary: The Numbers

- Research all of the costs of being in business that are necessary, regardless of the number of sales.

- Select a price point.

- Research the direct cost of delivering One Sale.

- Calculate the profit margin of One Sale by subtracting the direct cost from the price.

- Calculate how many One Sales are required to break even by dividing the costs of being in business by the margin of One Sale.

CHAPTER FOUR:
PERSONAL FIT

The Third Test Stage

So, you've passed the first and second test stages in the Idea Tester framework. Congratulations. We'll now move on to the third stage of testing. Recall from Table A that this stage is given a 40% weighting in the overall testing framework. As a reminder of how much time to commit to each section of this stage, part of Table A has been replicated below.

Table F   Personal Fit Framework

Test Stage Weighting	Stage Sections	Suggested Time Commitment
Personal Fit (40%)	Your Passion	1%
	Self-Analysis	30%
	Salary Expectations	14%
	Work-Life Balance	50%
	Test	5%
	Total	100%

When interviewing candidates for a new job, recruiters look for a good "fit" with the company. If that were not the case, then people would be hired based on their resume alone (which would be a relief to most of us who don't exactly love job interviews!). It is the personality fit that is most important. This can only be discovered through personal interactions. Will the new employee fit into the group, the division, the company?

It shouldn't be any different with your own company! **You** need to fit into this company just as much as any other. You **are** the company.

The basis for a good fit is being passionate about your idea and your own business. For an excellent fit, a few other central parts of your life should be aligned.

What is the ideal fit when it comes to your business idea? There must be a match between the components of the business and your:

- Values and passion
- Strengths and weaknesses
- Salary expectations and the financial rewards offered through the opportunity
- View of work-life balance and the amount of time that you are intending to work

Let's explore these parts of your life to ensure that the idea is not merely financially feasible, but is **perfect for you**.

Your Passion

It's that happy feeling you get when you see someone you "click" with, when you wear your favourite outfit, or do an activity you love. The French have a phrase, *je ne sais quoi*, which translates to something close to 'a certain unexplainable something.' This is the indefinable quality I'm talking about.

Of course, the first benefit of having this *je ne sais quoi* is that you will be much happier following your passion. The old adage, Do something you like and the money will follow, has been proven time and again.

Why does passion only constitute 1% of the time commitment for this chapter? It isn't necessarily that the other sections take longer to complete, it's that your passion should be obvious once you find it. It is similar to knowing that you are in love – you shouldn't need to question it.

You see that person on TV, at school, at work, in the coffee shop with whom you want to be friends. What is it about them? Is it money? Material things? The fact that they glow and radiate positive energy? More than likely, it is this last reason. Although you can envy the material things, it is this energy that draws people, and this energy comes from being passionate about what he or she does.

Just think about how differently you behave when you are doing things you are passionate about. What is the difference between someone who is really into playing hockey and someone who just enjoys it? The difference is huge! The passionate player tries for every single free puck, he doesn't hold back on his shots, and he puts 110% into everything else he does on the ice. Guess who is the team captain, and the player the team turns to for inspiration.

When people are excited about what they are doing, they radiate positive energy. Somehow, this attracts people. During the start of my own business, I noticed that strangers began talking to me out of the blue for some "unknown reason." This hadn't happened to me before. Passion is contagious.

"Listen to your heart!"

To run your own business and to get your idea off the ground, you will need the help of other people. If you love what you are doing, interfacing with others will be easier.

So what is your passion?

Passion has two drivers:

1. Avoiding negative things that you find disagreeable. Be true to yourself and stick to your values.

2. Doing things that positively motivate you or that you find exciting.

Let's discuss these in greater detail.

1. Reduce Negative Energy

Stay away from things that create negative energy in your life. Don't do things that go against your core values.

How do you do this?

- First, outline what your values are. Do they include honesty, kindness, understanding, friendliness, optimism, strength, integrity, openness, empathy? If you don't determine your spectrum of values, then you'll never have a baseline with which to assess whether an action is good or bad. By clearly laying out your values in advance, you prevent yourself from doing things that make you uncomfortable or that you know to be unethical. The best business people have both high moral standing and integrity.

- Second, ask yourself, how does your business embody those values? Make sure that you protect your business' integrity. Ensure that your personal values are fully ingrained within your company. It is best to write down your values and have them visible in your place of business. Your every action should support these values.

By creating a solid foundation both for yourself and your company, you will be able to mitigate negative energy.

2. Create Positive Energy

Passion is the best driver that an entrepreneur can have. If an individual absolutely loves what he or she is doing, then it does not feel like work. The goal here is to be so engaged in your work that when you finally look up at the clock, it's time to go home.

If you are nervous about starting your business and very unsure whether or not this is a good idea, ask yourself if you are genuinely enthusiastic enough to pursue this idea. Maybe wait for the next idea that you really believe in and are even more excited about.

A word of caution: on the flip side, being overly excited about the idea could blind you to the realities of the situation. The Idea Tester is a great tool and framework, but it won't do what it is supposed to do if you don't have an objective view of your idea. If you are already so excited about your business idea and can't imagine it not working out perfectly, you need to find yourself a devil's advocate.[15] The good news is that if you can convince the devil's advocate that your idea can fly – it probably can.

Quick & Easy Summary: Passion

- Passion is contagious.

- Passion draws people to you, makes them like you, and makes them want to help you.

- All the best business people have a high level of integrity.

- Build integrity by reducing negative energy, sticking to your values and having character.

- Do what you love and the money will follow.

- Ensure that someone around you plays the devil's advocate to prevent your passion from leading you astray.

---

15 A devil's advocate will critically and objectively analyze your idea. Traits you should look for in a devil's advocate:

- Someone who is realistic. Stay clear of people with pessimistic or optimistic overtones.

- Someone with an extremely high level of integrity, to protect your intellectual property.

- Someone who is comfortable with conflict or has a close enough relationship with you to be honest.

Self-Analysis

Everyone has natural strengths and weaknesses. Just as one man's junk is another man's treasure, one man's strengths can complement another man's weaknesses. Being self-aware is important.

Once you understand your capabilities and limitations, you will need to determine the following:

- Will your business **have** the skills required to produce your offering on site with in-house employees?
- Will you **learn** these skills?
- Will you **outsource** them to another company?[16]

Just like business costs, certain talents are a basic requirement for your business. When assessing the cost of being in business, a lack of start-up money would mean having to walk away from a business idea. Similarly, if you don't have the necessary skills and you can't get them, your idea is infeasible.

Performing a skills inventory is the first step in determining if you meet your business' skill requirements. Filling in the gaps is the second step.

Skills

There are two types of skills that must be analyzed to determine if the idea will fly.

1. Personal Self-Assessment
Skills and traits necessary to be an entrepreneur

---

16 Outsourcing is the new black. In the past, most companies believed that their entire business had to be performed internally. But why do that when another company performs the service that much better? Having another company do part of your business is called outsourcing. It adds more value to your customers, often costs less than doing it in-house, and the supplying company is responsible for keeping themselves best-in-class. Reap the benefits. It also only costs what you use, so it reduces risk and frees up cash. Some common things to outsource are computer services, recruitment, training, customer service, and marketing.

2. Business Skills Analysis
Skills necessary to run a business

"What skills do you have?"

Personal Self-Assessment

The harsh reality is that starting your own business is not easy. There is risk, it is scary, your budget changes significantly, your personal life becomes business-oriented, and you can't sleep because you are thinking about the next steps you need to take.

There are positives. There must be, or you wouldn't be thinking about launching your idea. Of course, there is the chance that your idea will sky rocket. There is also the flexibility and control to do exactly what you want.

But can **you** do it?

There is no "perfect" entrepreneur. Entrepreneurs come in all shapes and sizes. But, realize that there are many traits that would be helpful. Some helpful skills for an entrepreneur are listed below.

- Multi-tasking
- Staying focused
- Can work alone
- Team player

- Planning skills
- Decision-making
- Budgeting skills
- Creativity
- Effective Communication
- Good listening
- Patience
- Initiative
- Organization
- Effective Networking
- High-level thinking
- External locus of control
- Management
- Leadership

As you go through this list, think of the following questions:

1. Which are your strengths versus your weaknesses?

2. Are you going to be able to compensate for these limitations?

3. How can you leverage your strengths?

These traits may be difficult to change, as some are very ingrained in who we are. If you do identify that you are weak in one area, being aware of this can help mitigate any negative effects.

Many of these skills have been traditionally viewed from the opposite perspective. For example, someone who is great at multi-tasking is not commonly someone who can remain focused. An entrepreneur is expected to be able to work alone and participate as a team member. As an entrepreneur, you really have to be everything to everyone at one time or another. Based on these criteria, it should come as no surprise that there is no perfect entrepreneur.

Partnership Parity: *Partnerships are often more successful than a sole proprietorship, as the two entrepreneurs have more complementary skills.*

Partners also support each other financially and emotionally through the initial start up. Of course, partnerships also have their downside, with the risk of personal conflict.

Business Skills Analysis

What skill sets are required to **run** your business? In the beginning, you are every division in the organization, which means that you must be able to do a whole host of things. You are the CEO, the accountant, the sales manager, and the janitor. You must be able to perform each role at a minimum standard in order to be successful.

Use the form below to help you identify the necessary skills for running your business. The skills outlined are necessary for managing almost **any** business. But, this is your idea and you need to customize this list for yourself.

Form 7   Business Skills Analysis

Business Skill	Have it = H Learn it = L Buy it = O	Name of Individual Responsible
Sales		
Marketing		
Technology		
Operations		
Accounting		
Legal		
Human Resources		
Other		

Sales

Everyone in the company should be part of the sales team. They should be living, breathing and thinking about selling the company's offering, day and night. If they do, then you have a large and formidable sales team. You really can't afford for them not to be committed to sales.

Marketing

This person should be someone with a passion for life, a great communicator who represents your company's look-and-feel.[17] You won't get your name out there or win business without this person. It is better if they understand your target customer extremely well. It's **best** if they **are** a member of your target customer group. That way, they'll understand your customers' needs perfectly.

Technology

In today's technologically savvy business environment, if you don't have someone who "gets it" – you're sunk.

Operations

This is the **core** of your business. If you don't have a solid core, you have nothing to sell. If you don't have a solid core, you have nothing in which to invest. Marketing and accounting would have a difficult time without solid operations. Someone in the business has to have ownership of the offering and how it is delivered to your customer.

Accounting

Due diligence up front will help in the long run. If you set up the books properly at the beginning, time will be saved in the end.

17 See footnote 11, page 41.

Legal

Absolutely everything a company does is affected by the legal environment. This is especially true at the beginning when you are dealing with partnership agreements, incorporation, customer contracts, employee contracts, and agreements with suppliers. The list goes on.

Human Resources

The truth is that people are becoming the only advantage most companies have. In a start-up business, good people are essential, as you can't afford to have a bunch of slackers. You need to recruit, train, motivate, and retain quality employees.

Other

When you are charging people for your offering, you have to be an expert in your field! This is part of your competitive edge. You must be able to do something better than everyone else.

If you are a software developer, it is important to have programmers. If you are a hair salon owner, it is important to have qualified hairdressers. This section must be customized to your industry. Ensure that you identify all of the necessary skills. Ask people whom you respect to contribute to the list. Ideas are best built by several people with different perspectives. Add these skills to Form 7.

Have It, Learn It or Buy It

Once you have identified all the necessary skills for success, the next step is to identify which ones you already **have** within your network – those of your partners, friends, family and yourself. Then determine which ones might involve either internal **training** or **outsourcing**.

Have It

Some questions you should ask yourself when assessing if you **have** these skills:

- Is this my core business?[18]
- Do I have these skills?
- How many people on my team have these skills?
- How do I keep these people on board?
- What is my back-up plan if they leave?

The skills that you already have access to are great! However, it might be wise to have more than one person on staff with that skill. This is vital for tasks which are part of your core business. When it comes to sales, ensure that your entire organization realizes that they are **all** in sales. Even though you have allocated the responsibility to one individual, it should be on everyone's minds. Be careful when considering the skills of your friends and family. You want to ensure that you maintain your relationships with them, so be considerate of their time and financial needs.

Will Have It (Learning)

Some questions you should ask yourself when assessing if you should **learn** these skills:

- Is this my core business?
- How many people need to have these skills and how many of those people require training?
- How much will this training cost in time and money?
- How do these people keep their skills current?

Learning is a viable solution when one does not have a skill already, but has the time and money to learn it. However,

---

18 Core business has also been called the competitive edge, core competencies, or competitive advantage. It is something your company does better than the competition, provides better than your suppliers, and is the reason you are in business. If you were not good at it, you would not be in business for long.

there will be a learning curve. You must realize that, once you invest in training, it is still possible for this individual to leave the organization. This is a waste of money and something **no** business can afford. If you do train one individual, try to distribute that learning throughout the organization or formalize the training (through training manuals, job shadowing, job sharing, lunch and learns, etc.).

Someone Else Has It (Outsourcing)

Some questions you should ask yourself when assessing if you should **outsource** these skills:

- Is this my core business?
- Are there suitable suppliers who can provide it more efficiently?
- Do I need to protect proprietary information?
- Is it important to remain at the leading edge?
- Is the industry experiencing rapid change?
- Do the skill advances change quickly (IT upgrades, social networking best practices, etc.)?
- Do I require the use of this skill regularly?

If a skill requires constant training and it is not a part of your core business, consider outsourcing. It is the service provider's job to keep updated. Outsourcing should only be done for non-core operations. For example, if you are a software development company, you should have the programmers in-house, but your customer service could be outsourced. Before outsourcing, ensure that you have thoroughly evaluated your potential suppliers. The added value of the supplier in terms of expertise and time saved must outweigh the cost. The new trend is toward offshore sourcing, and in this situation, understanding your total costs becomes even more important.[19] Remember to protect your intellectual property to avoid creating a competitor. Finally, if you are only using a skill every few weeks, the total cost of outsourcing is less than having it in-house.

Assign someone on your management team or within your network of associates to be responsible for each skill. Form 7 will help you organize this. They must have it, plan on learning it in the short-term, or have the contacts to outsource responsibly for it. This creates a clear map in your head of what is required and how you will obtain it. In today's competitive business environment, having good people with the necessary skill sets is often the only sustainable competitive advantage that a company has.

Note: About Knowledge Management

Knowledge management is the capturing of the company data held in employees' heads.

The term "knowledge management" is a **huge** buzz phrase that has emerged, due to the importance of capturing and sharing knowledge throughout ever-growing companies. People who have worked at a company for twenty-five years have knowledge inside their heads that is not written down anywhere. When they leave the company, the knowledge leaves with them. This knowledge has the potential to be extremely valuable.

Some examples of knowledge within a company that could be lost without proactive knowledge management:

- Contacts with suppliers, customers, and industry people which have been developed over the years

---

19 Offshore sourcing is when a company goes outside of the local region to purchase supplies, raw materials, or any supplementary service. The rationale is that a country specializing in one specific offering would be able to provide it better than local companies, especially with technology improvements and standardization of government policies. The book, *The World is Flat*, by Thomas Friedman, speaks extensively about this phenomenon, while companies such as Elance, craigslist, Alibaba, and Li & Fung have been capitalizing on it.

- The history of these contacts, their opinions and mutual jokes which have been the basis for relationships
- The learning curve of knowing whom to call when things go bad – the first time
- The learning curve of getting a task done in the quickest way possible
- The inherent know-how of seeing tell-tale signs to enable good decisions
- How to best deal with quirky customer requests

Large organizations are evaluating their internal strengths every time they deal with succession planning, training and development, targeting new business opportunities and deciding when to outsource specific activities. Because the start-up company has a tiny workforce, evaluating your current skills and required knowledge is more basic. The company might be just you. You don't have to train anyone else!

It is still important for start-up businesses to begin considering knowledge management for the following reasons:

1. If you are the entrepreneur, you don't want **everyone** in your company coming to you for **every question**. What a waste of precious time that would be! By creating standard documentation, training, and creating a vision to guide employee actions, you are empowering them.

2. As the company grows, employees need a way to link to each other. In some larger companies, tenure and political power is derived from knowing the right person to seek out for information. New employees stay in entry-level positions for twelve months, and arguably what they learn is where to find people in the organization. Most companies don't expect value from a new employee for six months to one year as they learn the lay of the land. Imagine how much more productive your business will be by planning for this at the outset!

Think about knowledge management at the beginning, and it will help you in the end.

Quick & Easy Summary: Self-Analysis

- Specific personal traits are required to be an entrepreneur. Not everyone is right for this role. Not everyone will enjoy it.

- Identify your competitive edge and the necessary skills to deliver it. Make sure that you have access to these skills.

- By listing the business skills necessary to be successful, you can make a plan either to have them, learn them, or outsource them.

Salary Expectations

This is a personal decision. **Be honest.** If you're not, you are only hurting yourself.

Each person's understanding of an "acceptable salary" varies tremendously, and can change dramatically over time. This variability makes the definition of a "successful business" radically different from individual to individual, as the desired profit varies.

Salary expectations are made up of three components:

1. The opportunity costs incurred
2. The individual's willingness to accept risk
3. The intrinsic value provided from pursuing one's passion

Unfortunately, most business plans do not take this into consideration. In fact, business plan financial details don't include the founder's salary as part of the expenses. It is assumed that the profits are the salary. This becomes problematic, as a typical small business doesn't make a profit in its first year of operation. How are you going to be able to pay the bills? Even when a business appears to be making money, the owner is living paycheck to paycheck, just like the rest of us. It's a good thing that this book is not like most business plans!

What is the income level that you would require in order to make this business a "success"? By considering this question up front, you can evaluate your idea against this parameter.

Opportunity Costs

An opportunity cost is the next best alternative to what you are currently doing. The time and money you spend working on one idea prevents you from realizing any positives from other ideas. If you are able to do multiple things at the same time (such as starting your business while maintaining a full-time job), there is no opportunity cost. However, your free time would be included in such costs. Common alternatives include:

- A job
- Pursuing other ideas
- Enjoying your free time

These are all legitimate opportunity costs of pursuing your idea.

Different individuals have different opportunity costs. For instance, a General Manager making $100,000 a year has a higher opportunity cost of leaving his job than the clerk making $40,000. Your expectations for future income are contingent on what you are currently making.

If you are like the General Manager with a salary of $100,000 per year, you would only leave this position if the financial reward of owning your own business was in a similar dollar range or offered significant intrinsic rewards.

Risk Factor

Willingness to take on risk is different among individuals. An individual who is comfortable with risk would require a smaller return on investment for taking that risk. His or her salary expectations would be lower, which means that more ideas will fit his or her personal expectations.

Factors which affect willingness to take on risk:

- **Stage of Life**
  The younger a person is, the easier it is for them to take on risk. A woman in her twenties is not investing her life savings in an idea. She perceives that she can always make that money back in the long run. Both of these forces reduce the negative backlash of losing everything.

  The interesting thing is that most people who start their own businesses don't do it early in life when they might have less to lose; many young people feel that they haven't acquired enough experience to start a business. Ironically, once they have the experience later in life, the risk factor has increased.

- **Dependents**

  There is the added risk that your decisions could negatively affect your loved ones as well as yourself. The number and type of dependents is most easily illustrated through the General Manager example. If the General Manager has a family to support, she will be less likely to assume the risk of quitting a job than the woman in her twenties without children (and possibly the option of moving back home).

- **Living Expenses** (and willingness to part with your standard of living!)

  Finally, the number of (fixed) living expenses increases risk. If you have a mortgage, student loans, cell phone contracts and so on, these all reduce the chance that you can accept the risk of minimal income for a period of time. The high school student who is working part-time during the summer while living at home has less risk than someone tied into multiple payment plans. Many of these fixed expenses could be forfeited (including the cell phone and a daily purchased lunch), but there is also the unwillingness to part with one's current standard of living. Even if one opts out of these fixed costs, there can be a tremendous negative impact. Not only are there cancellation fees that come into play, but you are going to fondly remember the "good old days" when you had a stable income. No wonder Canadians are so risk adverse!

There is one more caveat – your salary expectations need to be higher than your salary requirements. Salary requirements are the minimum level that you can accept. You need to eat, sleep, and pay for other basics. You need to do a budget of your fixed expenses to make sure that you salary is above this threshold.

It is expected by many entrepreneurs that the first few years are not going to be profitable, but there is the potential for long-term financial return. So, it is also a good idea for you to know the number of months that you can survive without any income.

Make sure that you can answer these questions to protect yourself:

- How much money do you have access to or have you saved for living expenses?
- What are your monthly living expenses?
- How many months will this money allow you to survive?
- Is this enough time to make things happen?

Once you factor in your risk components, you may realize that your salary expectations are higher or lower than you thought. What are you willing to give up? What can you put on the line?

Intrinsic Value

There are huge benefits to having your own company!

Some entrepreneurs prefer to be their own bosses, have control, and do what they are passionate about. The desired income level is actually less than what they might currently be making if employed by a company.

But, it would be a lie to say that being an entrepreneur is all glamour. It can be an emotional rollercoaster; it can be lonely, tiring, and unending. You get the point. For some people, this is part of the entrepreneur experience; for others, this takes away their love of the business.

The Real Break-Even Point

Remember – Be honest!

Once you understand what you are looking for as a financial reward, you will be better able to determine whether starting your own business and pursuing this idea is feasible for **you**.

> Opportunity Cost
> + Risk Factor
> - Intrinsic Rewards
> = Salary Expectations

What are your salary expectations? Write them down!

"Write them down!"

Will this idea meet your salary expectations?

Your salary was not included in the costs of being in business when computing the initial break-even point. Why? We had to test the **idea's** feasibility before trying to fit it into **your** life. Now your salary expectations are front and centre!

There are two separate concepts to examine here:

1. The costs of being in business must be covered in order for this idea to be feasible.
2. The start-up costs **plus your salary expectations** must be covered in order for this idea to be **worth your while**. Only then will you be enticed to quit your job (or other distractions) and commit to the idea.

The real break-even analysis allows you to identify not only how many One Sales you need to cover your costs, but how many are required to be a "success," and to generate the income you desire. The formula is as simple as the previous break-even formula.

Real Break-Even Point =
(Cost of Being in Business + Salary Expectations) / Margin per One Sale

---

If the real break-even number of One Sales is unreasonable, this business plan will not live up to **your expectations**. You may consider re-adjusting your salary expectations or you may decide that the idea is not worth pursuing.

Note: About Taxes

You might have noticed that I've ignored something that is as inevitable as death… Taxes. I've ignored taxes for one fundamental reason – every entrepreneur aspires to pay taxes. I once heard AJ Virmanj (founder and owner of Cargo Jet) say that paying taxes means that you are making money, which is the point of starting a business. If you are truly worried about the impact of taxes, use the following formula to determine your after-tax salary expectations and re-calculate your real break-even target.

> Salary Expectations after-tax =
> Salary Expectations / (1 + personal income tax rate %)

Quick & Easy Summary: Salary

- Your salary expectations are dictated by other opportunities available to you, your willingness to take on risk, and your personal intrinsic rewards.

- The next best opportunities that could increase your salary expectations include other jobs, other ideas, or your free time. Do **not** overlook the value of free time.

- Willingness to take on risk can depend on your stage of life, your dependents, and your fixed living expenses.

- Intrinsic rewards can reduce your salary expectations significantly.

- Just paying off your start-up costs means the **idea** works.

- Paying off your start-up costs and salary expectations means you can **go**!

Work-Life Balance

Is "work-life balance" only a buzz phrase? I used to think so, but after living in Vancouver for the last 3 years, I started realizing that it might actually be a way of life. I no longer mind waiting in lines; I don't get angry sitting in traffic.

I live for the journey, rather than the destination.

Often an entrepreneur's physical presence is required by the business, forcing them to work sixty- to eighty-hour work-weeks, indefinitely. In fact, "work-life balance" and "be your own boss" are two phrases which, in the past, have been mutually exclusive.

The Idea Tester helps you to have your cake and eat it too. By setting work-life balance parameters up front, the business model is designed to meet these choices.

The key to having work-life balance is the idea that all things are good in moderation. Although starting a new business might be important to an entrepreneur, this is not the complete dream. Entrepreneurs still want time alone and time socializing with friends and family.

How much time are you willing to put in? Be honest.

Being extremely honest about how much you are willing to work means you can develop a business which matches your goals, both financial and personal. If you determine that your business idea demands too much of your time, at least it is preferable to discover this before leaving your job. This prevents you from succumbing to the old "the grass is always greener" phenomenon. Although having your own business sounds good, if you only want to work thirty-five hours a week with lunch and coffee breaks, don't quit the day job.

This section will establish the time you will need to spend at work by going through these three components:

1. Time Required to Deliver One Sale

Determine how much time a typical One Sale takes to deliver.

2. Capacity

Calculate how many One Sales can be done with your current staff.

3. Utilization

Out pops how much of your day is going to be spent doing tasks directly related to reaching your real break-even goal.

1. Time to Deliver One Sale

There is so much involved in running a business, from sales to administrative work. What we need to find out in this section is how much additional time each One Sale will take to deliver in full to a customer. This includes all the customer interactions, including any activity that is done once an additional single sale is made.

Process mapping can determine how much time a One Sale takes.[20] "Yuck!" you say. Okay. I like process mapping, but for those who are not business majors, this may be a scary term.

Process mapping is easy. An example of a process might be the steps involved in running a coffee shop, from taking a customer's order, to giving them a steaming cup of coffee. The important part is to identify all of the steps in between. Each step takes time. In the coffee shop example, the customer has to decide what they want, the clerk has to determine the price, the customer pays, and the clerk gets the food and makes the drink. The customer might ask additional questions or need a napkin. All of these steps in the process take staff time.

It is a little more difficult to judge how much time a product process takes. You might think that a customer buying a product involves little or no company time. In the case of purchasing and distributing a product from China directly to a customer location, it is especially difficult to assess the time taken for each sale. Another example might

---

20 Process mapping is the visual display of how something is done. An example is the customer order at McDonald's:

Smile and Greet Customer > Take Order >
Make Food > Package Food > Accept Payment

be the limited work involved in online sales. The product doesn't even come through your place of business! How does it take time?

For each new One Sale, there is still customer service or a sales cycle, which all take time. If you assess this sale as zero minutes, not only will it not give you any information for the test, but it is unlikely to be accurate. It almost always takes **some** time. Even an online application might have an average number of customer service calls or invoicing setup requirements. If there isn't a specific and direct amount of time for each customer, an average works well. The good news is that if you believe that there is little work to be done, your idea is most likely scalable.

The process to deliver a customer One Sale may be complicated or extremely simple. The time commitment to deliver a customer One Sale may be short or long. Processes and times are varied!

You need to determine what customer interactions are part of a typical customer sale. This includes the sales time, data inputting, delivery time, etc. The more sales you have, the more time you will spend doing these tasks. So, we can call them "variable tasks."

There are some other benefits you can realize through process mapping:

- Continuous improvement initiatives[21]
- Creation of training documents
- An expedited learning curve

So let's map your process by listing all of the tasks and the time each task takes for each additional One Sale. Form 8 is designed to help you through this process.

Task

A task is one of the steps that are involved in the process. Each task should take a specific amount of time.

---

21 Continuous improvement is the mentality in a business to constantly pursue perfection in terms of process improvement, in an attempt to generate more customer value. What a mouthful! Basically, most companies record when things go wrong and then come up with a way to prevent that from happening again.

Time

After identifying all of the time-consuming, customer-related variable tasks, it is important to allocate an amount of time for each task. Although all customers are different and tasks can have variable times, you need to estimate. Below is a sample task sheet. Your business will have different tasks.

Form 8   Time to Deliver a "One Sale"

Task	Time (minutes)
Sales	
Qualify	
Negotiate	
Manufacturing	
Packaging	
Shipping	
Invoicing	
Total Time	

2. Capacity

Now you realize how much time it takes to deliver One Sale. With this knowledge, we have the first piece of information necessary to determine your capacity at its current resource level. Basically, it answers the question, how many One Sales you can perform at your current employee level?

How do you find out your capacity?

You need to figure out **how many resources** you have for the time period which you are monitoring (this includes your time too!). This is done by multiplying the number of employees working at the business by the number of hours that they work. This must be for the same time period that you are monitoring your real break-even point by.

For example, if you are tracking real break-even One Sale targets on an annual basis, you need to determine your hours of work for the year. On the other hand, if it is important to know what your daily real break-even target was, then your hours available should be daily.

For your own hours, you must be extremely honest about the amount of time that you are willing to put in. Is it eight hours a day? Or only four? What does your typical work day/week look like? A paralegal must be available for court dates. A coffee shop sells most cups of coffee in the morning. Conversely, a computer programmer can work when they like.

If your business employs yourself and multiple employees, what is the average day of work? For example, if you have two employees who each work two thousand hours per year, and you intend on working two thousand hours per year, your resources available will be six thousand hours per year (3 workers x 2,000 hours = 6,000 hours).

To be more accurate, you could reduce your resources available by 25% to reflect that the workforce is only performing productive work 75% of the time. This is more realistic, as few employees work productively for their entire shifts. The formula to calculate capacity can be done by different time periods (by day, week, month or year). Just be sure to consistently substitute in the time period.

By knowing how many resources you have, you now know how much time is available to perform multiple One Sales. This means that you can now determine your capacity with the following formula.

Capacity for One Sales =
Resources Available (hours) / Time to Deliver One Sale

Example:

You are a newsletter designer who only wants to work four days per week for eight hours. If a newsletter takes you sixteen hours to create, you can only create two newsletters per week. You have reached capacity at this point. Capacity limits how much profit you can make.

Maximum One Sales per Week = (# employees x average working hours per week) / time to deliver a One Sale

employees = 1 (yourself, the designer)
Average working hours per week = 4 days by 8 hours = 32 hours per week
Time to deliver a One Sale = 16 hours

Maximum One Sales per Week = (1 x 32) / 16 = 2

Time Tip: *This information is automatically calculated at www.makeitfly.ca when you fill out the Idea Tester online.*

---

3. Utilization

Once you determine how many One Sales can be performed in a specified time frame, you see how much of your time will be necessary to meet your financial goals. After achieving the number of One Sales required to meet your real break-even target, how much time is remaining?

The simple calculation for this time factor is:

% Utilization =
(Real Break-Even Target / Capacity of One Sales) x 100

*Make sure that you are using the same time period in order to compare apples to apples. If your real break-even target is measured in weeks, your capacity should also be measured in weeks.

Let's continue the example of the newsletter designer. If you are only able to create two newsletters per week, but need to design three newsletters per week in order to reach your real break-even target, then this idea is infeasible (the % utilization would be (3 / 2) x 100 = 150%). You will have to work longer hours, charge more, or change your salary expectations for this idea to give you the work-life balance you seek.

Time Tip: Again, this is automatically calculated at www.makeitfly.ca when you fill out the Idea Tester online.

Now you know how much time each day you have to work before you reach your target. Is it more than you thought it would be? Is it less? Let's break down the test results:

Ugly

If utilization is larger than 100%, you need to automate a task, cut out a task, work more, hire more people or contract something out. Of course, if you work more, your work-life balance will suffer. If you hire more employees or contract work out, your costs change. Make sure that you adjust the model to reflect this!

Bad

If utilization is 100%, that means that you are working the **entire** day to meet the real break-even target. The higher the utilization rate, the busier you and your employees will be. Remember that you only have 24 hours in the day and most people require sleep!

Good

If your utilization rate is less than 100%, this is good. But, make sure that it is not too close to 100%. Remember, this is just the time that it takes to do the "variable tasks" which are contingent on the number of sales. There are also a whole host of "fixed tasks" that you need time to do. These include payroll (without which your employees will leave), accounting (without which you won't be able to keep track of your sales), taxes (without which you may go to jail) and marketing (without which there are NO sales!). It is important that your utilization is low enough to allow you the extra time to do these other things.

You can now see why so many entrepreneurs work sixty to eighty hours per week. It is my hope that by realizing the time commitment up front, you'll be able to cut out the non-value-adding tasks and determine when you need more resources (and whether or not you can afford them!).

Great

A utilization rate under 30% is great! This is especially true for a new business, since it is important to spend considerable time marketing and setting up. Remember that things always take longer than you expect. Here is a list of some things that may creep up that you hadn't expected:

- Fixing mistakes and starting at the bottom of the learning curve
- Meeting with people, including travel time
- Marketing initiatives, including networking, seminars, press releases, etc.
- Personal obligations that come up

This Is The Advanced Stuff (Completely Optional!)

Why else is it important to know your **capacity**? There are a few different uses for this number:

- You are able to see what your maximum revenue could be at this resource level. This can be done by taking the capacity and multiplying it by your price.

> Maximum Revenue at Resource Level =
> Capacity x Price per One Sale

- You can monitor your sales to determine when you need to add more staff. If you have more sales than capacity, you need to hire more people.

- You can determine how much free time your staff have. You can figure out how many hours your staff are working by multiplying the current sales volume by the time to deliver a One Sale. Their free time is then easily calculated by subtracting their working time from the capacity.

> Free Time =
> Capacity – (Current Sales Volume x Time to Deliver a One Sale)

Quick & Easy Summary: Work-Life Balance

- All things are good in moderation and you will be happier in the long run if understand this from the beginning.

- By figuring out how much time a customer sale takes, you can determine steps that can be eliminated, automated, or improved upon.

- Utilization is the amount of capacity spent to meet real break-even requirements. If this result is over 30%, it may be difficult to get all your other work done in the time you want.

Personal Fit Test

Is there an excellent fit between your values, passion, strengths, salary expectations, and work-life balance?

If not, there are still things to consider:

1. **Have you chosen an industry that presents an opportunity based on your values, passion, and personal strengths? Or merely one that presents challenges?**

   There may be a huge opportunity to take your idea and adjust it slightly to a different target market. This fine-tuning of your idea may take full advantage of your true passion. If you have come up with a service for accounting firms, but your true passion is snowboarding, take a second look at the idea to see if something in the idea is transferable.

   There is a chance that your business situation looks like an uphill battle, but maybe it is just a very difficult industry to enter. In this case, it would be extremely difficult for other competitors to enter the market also, especially if you have a first-mover advantage.[22] Even though the obstacles appear insurmountable, your business idea might still be viable.

2. **Are your salary expectations so high that your costs become insurmountable?**

   Your living expenses may simply be too high. If you really love this business idea, you might have to take a very serious look at your living expenses and live by a strict budget. You might end up having to forgo lunch at the cafeteria, or give up that gym membership. Consider cheaper alternatives, like packing your lunch, and jogging outdoors. Sometimes money-saving changes, like cutting back on cigarettes, might end up being

---

22 A first-mover advantage is when a company delivers a solution to the target market before competitors. People are naturally risk adverse. Customers don't like changing, giving the first provider an advantage. They would have to do something poorly in order for the customer to actively seek an alternative.

positive for your health. You have to decide what is more important to you – having your own company or maintaining your standard of living.

3. Can anything in the process be cut out?

If your time utilization was too high, then you have a few options that you can consider to make this idea work:

- You might have enough margin to hire an additional worker, freeing up your time for other things. You'll also find possibilities in internships, co-ops, volunteer work, family help, and temporary workers.
- You could contract work out.
- You may be able to automate a step in the process.
- You could take out any steps in the customer process which don't add value to the customer.

If this test proves that your idea might not fly… STOP!

If this test proves that it might be easier than you thought possible… GO! GO! GO!

Quick & Easy Summary: Personal Fit

- Passion cannot be made, bought, or sold. You have it or you don't. And you **need** to be passionate about your own business.

- Know your own values and infuse them into your business.

- Your salary expectations should take into account other opportunities that you forgo, your willingness to take on risk, and any additional intrinsic rewards.

- Your salary expectations will change how many One Sales must be generated in order for your business to be a "success."

- Formalize your service process – this is the beginning of continuous improvement in your business.

• Determine how much you have to work to just meet sales targets and make sure that you have time for administrative work, networking, sales initiatives, and things that may take longer than expected.

CHAPTER FIVE:
FIND YOUR NICHE

Now What?

The test is over. Did your idea pass?

This chapter is a **bonus** chapter. It is related to the Idea Tester, as it is a key element for moving forward.

Once you have decided to move forward, the biggest challenge seems to be figuring what to do next. Where do you focus your time? In fact, Andrew Patricio, the CEO and founder of BizLaunch.ca (a company which hosts seminars for start-up companies), has said that the difference between a tremendously successful company versus a mediocre one is its ability to target the customer. The niche. An optimal niche is a group of customers with **commonalities** who have a **need for your offering**, but that **need is only being partially met** by the competition.

Let's break this definition down and provide some examples.

A "**commonality**" among customers could be:

- **Where They Live**
  Does your product only lend itself to a certain geographical location, or are you able to provide long-distance service, even across borders? If you were a local mechanic, you would focus on local customers. You need them to get their cars to you because you can't move your shop.

- **What They Do with Their Time**
  Time can be further segmented as either the customers' free time or time at work. Lulu Lemon has targeted people who are active and enjoy yoga. This allows them to offer valuable information and products which target this lifestyle.

- **Their Values or Beliefs**
  Corporate social responsibility and sustainability are all hot topics these days that your company can tap into. Be careful that you practice only what you preach; customers are wary of misrepresentation and dislike having the wool pulled over their eyes. If your customer group is active in environmental causes, then you should consider having a green product.

- **Other**
  This is any other criterion that you can identify as separating this group from their peers. You'd be surprised at how some companies describe their target markets. Some may be for young males aged twelve to twenty-five, whereas others are so detailed that they are able to draw a picture of their ideal customer.

A "**need for your offering**" is usually reinforced as the target customers are currently purchasing the product from the competition. To determine the willingness to purchase, the best method is to actually know that they **already** purchase elsewhere.

That their "**needs are only being partially met**" merely indicates you realize that the target customer has multiple needs, but the competition's offering only satisfies a few of them.

An example is a businessman who enjoys a beer after work. If he is in the niche that drinks beer to relax at home, he wants a product that won't break the bank. Most domestic beers go after this market. The man might also be concerned that he has to finish some work from the office **and** he is worried about his waistline. This is why Coors Light has been able to satisfy more needs than other common domestic beers.

The rest of the chapter will cover:

1. The advantages of targeting a niche market
2. How to select a niche market

This has everything to do with whether or not your idea will fly!

Why Niche Markets?

Always focus.

In the first section, you outlined the need, the offering and how the offering was unique. Since then, you have confirmed that the idea makes sense financially and works well with your lifestyle. However, have you narrowed it down to one concept?

It sounds silly, but having one business idea does not necessarily mean that you have focused. Not at all. If you have a great idea, there are still umpteen directions that you could go in with it.

- You could sell the offering online and sell it to more technologically savvy customers.
- You could sell it locally and only focus on people connected to your community.
- You could sell it nationally to customers who have the same requirements as you.
- You could sell it internationally to customers who have never seen this type of product before.

Unfortunately, if you haven't decided on one direction, then you still won't know where to start.

Most entrepreneurs find this out the hard way, myself included. I remember clearly the day I realized that I was offering **ten** different services and, consequently, would find it nearly impossible to sell any one.

The interesting thing – you haven't changed your idea. You just haven't decided to whom you should sell it.

Ensure that you are focused on **one product** being delivered to **one customer** with a **specific need**. All too often, entrepreneurs are unfocused and try to be everything to everyone. As a small business owner, you are willing to do almost anything for cash flow. A good analogy is that of a machine gun versus a sniper rifle. The reality is that you are a very small company and do not have the resources to be everything to everyone. Focus.

Focus helps you to:

1. Customize your offering to more fully meet the customers' needs.
2. Minimize your marketing costs, as marketing is used only in locations or through mediums that reach the target customer, rather than in mass media.
3. Maximize your marketing benefits, since the message is tailored to your customers, and speaks meaningfully to its recipients.

How Do You Focus?

You have to choose which customer need/offering pairing is the best way to go.

What is a need/offering pairing? In Chapter Two, we started with a need and then developed an offering for that need. Later in the chapter, we discussed how an offering can be developed to fulfill multiple needs. Once we understand that different target markets have different needs, we realize that they need different offerings. This is one of the main reasons that companies have so many different product offerings – they are trying to meet the needs of multiple target markets.

Since it is inadvisable for you to go to the mass market and satisfy all needs at once, you are faced with a conundrum. You have a great idea, but this idea could be tweaked for different customer markets. These customer markets are different, based on the total offering and the specific customer need being met.

What do you do? This section contains a five-step process to help you determine which target markets are the best to pursue.

Step 1: List All Potential Need/Offering Pairings

List all customer needs related to your idea and match them to an offering that you could provide. Make sure that you list all possible channels. If you miss one now, you will spend time later either regretting it or reconsidering what route you should have chosen. **Both are a waste of time.**

Form 9: Customer Need/Offering

Option	Customer Need	Offering
A		
B		
C		
D		
E		

Step 2: Realize That You Have to Choose

You must choose.

If you don't, your marketing efforts will be ineffective. You are essentially wasting money. (As an entrepreneur, you can't afford to do this!)

Alternatively, and equally as bad, you won't start moving forward, since you will continue to struggle with finding a direction. By taking the time to select the customer who best matches your business, you are, in effect, saving time. Select multiple need/offerings only if you need them to reasonably meet your break-even targets.

Step 3: Evaluate the Options

How do you choose? Leverage what is in place by finding the best fit between yourself, your company and the customers' needs.[23] If you are extremely good at applying make-up, you enjoy making people feel pretty, and there aren't any make-up artists in your community, you can leverage these existing factors.

What is required for a good fit with your customer? A few things should be leveraged:

1. Your strengths
2. Weak competition
3. A lucrative market
4. Ease of marketing
5. Your passion (again!)

Not all of these categories may be equally important to you. You could give one category more weight than the others.

---

23 Leverage is the act of using something that you already have or that is already in existence in order to get even better results. It is taking advantage of a good situation. If you are carrying a ball down a hill, why not leverage gravity to help you with that by rolling it on the ground instead?

Your Strengths

Your strength or expertise will determine the best product/ service you can offer. Go with what you know. If you have the most experience in dyeing hair — be the colorist. That makes more sense than going up against the top hairdresser for a client. Not only will past employers be willing to give you excellent recommendations, but these customer testimonials in a specific area will grow fast. Build from a solid foundation.

Weak Competition

Customers are more likely to switch to your company because the competition is weak or does not meet their needs entirely. An easy way to test this is to determine what your competition looks like within a narrower scope. A good example is in the paralegal business. Few paralegals actively seek out clients requiring representation for driving or parking tickets. If they did, it would be an uphill battle, since there are companies that have strategically positioned themselves as traffic ticket specialists. Once a niche market has been captured by someone else, it is usually best to turn your attention elsewhere — unless you are able to meet the target market's needs more fully.

A Lucrative Market

The money that you make in this endeavor should be lucrative. The best way to judge profitability is to figure out all of the products/services that you could offer. Then, figure out how much margin you make from each and how long each takes to deliver. By dividing the price of the offering by the number of hours required to deliver it, you'll determine your hourly wage. With an hourly wage, you can objectively compare your offerings for their profitability.

For example, you are a mechanic offering brakes and oil changes. If a brake job takes you two hours and your profit margin is $100, you are making $50 per hour ($100 / 2 =

$50). In comparison, an oil change takes twenty minutes and your profit margin is $20, then you are making $60 per hour ($20 x 3 = $60). When comparing these two service offerings, oil changes are more lucrative.

Form 10 provides a template for you to determine the profitability of each offering objectively.

Form 10   Hourly Wage

	Offering	Margin / One Sale	Time (Hours)	Margin / Time = Hourly Wage
1				
2				
3				
4				
5				
6				

Go for the customer that helps your business succeed. With more money in your pocket, you'll have momentum and a solid business foundation. Eventually, this will allow you to go after another niche market, and keep growing from your foundation.

Ease of Marketing

This is the ability to reach your target audience. Do you have the contacts to reach the top management at a few key companies? Do you have a lot of friends in a particular industry? The key factor is to choose a target audience that is easy to reach. You'll need contacts or a network within the industry. The target audience should all read the same magazine, or share other habits. If they are a very select group, it may be easiest just to give them a shout via telephone.

Your Passion

Surprise – Here it is again! Passion.

If you do what you are enthusiastic about, you will make money. You will also be happier – which is worth a lot.

Step 4: Compare

Now compare your need/offering pairings as objectively as possible. Remember, be honest.

Form 11 has been designed to make this as easy as possible, but it might help to have a calculator beside you.

Here is how you should use this form:

1. First, list all of the need/offering pairings in the offering column.
2. Next, for each need/offering pairing, establish a value between 1 and 5 for the impact that each leverage category will have on the success of your business if you were to pursue that pairing (1 being a Slightly Positive Impact and 5 being a Very Positive Impact).
3. Once you have established the impact value of each leverage category for all need/offering pairings, you add them up and enter the result in the Total column.
4. Each need/offering pairing has a score that can be easily compared.

Form 11   Niche Selection

	Offering	Your Strengths	Weak Competition	Lucrative Market	Ease of Marketing	Passion	Total
1							
2							
3							
4							
5							
6							

By ranking your need/offering pairings using these factors, you will be able to better determine which niche market to start with.

Step 5: Stick to It

Nothing happens immediately. It takes multiple interactions with customers and countless marketing initiatives to get your message across to customers. With people being bombarded by thousands of marketing messages each year, is it any wonder that yours doesn't make it through the first time?

You need to give this strategy time. Make sure that you can survive for a certain period of time without cash flow.

Quick & Easy Summary: Find Your Niche

- Focus on one specific offering for one specific target market.

- Tailor your offerings as much as possible to the specified target market.

- Choose a target market which both is profitable and leverages your strengths and passion, while exploiting weak competition and open communication channels.

CHAPTER SIX:
NEXT STEPS

Will It Really Fly?

It looks like your idea stands a real chance if it has passed all the previous tests. This chapter helps you to reframe your thoughts and review what you have just covered in all of the previous chapters. It will also set you up with a solid plan for moving forward.

Review

The Idea Tester posed you a lot of tough questions!

1. Is there a genuine need to be fulfilled and does your offering meet that need better than the available alternatives?

2. Will this idea make enough money to cover all of the costs involved in being in business?

3. Is there an excellent fit between your values, passion, strengths, salary expectations, and work-life balance?

The book can be summarized with the following key take-away points.

Your Idea

- To start, you need a product/service concept which includes a specific business model.

- All great ideas start with a need and end in an offering.

- An offering should be a mix of both products and services which add value to the customer.

- Your offering must be different from your competitors' and difficult to duplicate in order to be successful.

The Numbers

- Research all of the costs of being in business that are necessary, regardless of the number of sales.

- Select a price point.

- Research the direct cost of delivering One Sale.

- Calculate the profit margin of One Sale by subtracting the direct cost from the price.

- Calculate how many One Sales are required to break even by dividing the costs of being in business by the margin of One Sale.

Personal Fit

- Passion cannot be made, bought, or sold. You have it or you don't. And you **need** to be passionate about your own business.

- Know your own values and infuse them into your business.

- Your salary expectations should take into account other opportunities that you forgo, your willingness to take on risk, and any additional intrinsic rewards.

- Your salary expectations will change how many One Sales must be generated in order for your business to be a "success."

- Formalize your service process – this is the beginning of continuous improvement in your business.

- Determine how much you have to work to just meet sales targets and make sure that you have time for administrative work, networking, sales initiatives, and things that may take longer than expected.

Your Niche

- Focus on one specific offering for one specific target market.

- Tailor your offerings as much as possible to the specified target market.

- Choose a target market which both is profitable and leverages your strengths and passion, while exploiting weak competition and open communication channels.

Now that you have learned how to test one idea, you can use this framework to test five ideas in record time. Just remember to follow the original time breakdown and the ground rules of the Idea Tester and you are set!

Table G   The Idea Tester Framework

Test Stage Weighting	Stage Sections	Suggested Time Commitment
Your Idea (25%)	Fulfilling a Need	25%
	Your Offering	20%
	Differentiation	50%
	Test	5%
	Total	100%

The Numbers (35%)	Cost of Being In Business	50%
	Profit Margin	30%
	Break-even Point	10%
	Test	10%
	Total	*100%*
Personal Fit (40%)	Your Passion	1%
	Self-Analysis	30%
	Salary Expectations	14%
	Work-Life Balance	50%
	Test	5%
	Total	*100%*

Business Strategy

Now is the time to create a business strategy to support your idea. Only your best ideas should make it to this phase.

The next steps should be a combination of:

- Gathering Market Research
- Learning
- Networking
- Writing Your Business Plan
- Creating An Action Plan
- Acting

Let's look at each of these steps in greater depth.

Gathering Market Research

The numbers worked, but now you need to verify your assumptions:

a. that there is a genuine need,
b. that your offering will satisfy that need,
c. that your market is large enough to meet your real break-even targets, and
d. that your sales projections are well-founded.

Learning

Continual learning will keep you ahead of the game. Make sure that you are working on the skills that you have identified as being necessary for your idea to be successful.

The trouble is that you often don't have time to do this. Always carry a book with you in case you find yourself waiting somewhere for a few minutes.

Networking

Meet as many people as possible and re-connect with old networks. A few keys to effective networking:

- Ask questions. Listening is more important than talking.
- Have a thirty-second pitch about your idea that is powerful and direct. It should include the need to be fulfilled and who has it, your offering, and how it is unique.
- Only go to networking events that have either potential partners or potential customers. These events cost you both time and money.

Writing Your Business Plan

Organize your thoughts, develop a strategy and build the tool that will help you apply for funding. Although the Idea Tester saves you time and money up front, there are still major benefits to eventually developing a formal business plan.

Helpful Links: Business Plan Templates

http://www.bdc.ca/en/business_tools/business_plan/default.
htm?cookie%5Ftest=1

http://www.bplans.com/sample_business_plans.cfm

http://www.canadabusiness.ca/servlet/ContentServer?cid=116001
9093568&lang=en&pagename=CBSC_NL%2Fdisplay&c=Guide
InfoGuide

Creating an Action Plan

Neither family members, friends, angel investors, venture capitalists, nor banks will give you any funding if you don't move ahead. First, plan how to proceed, and then take **action**.

If you fail to plan, you plan to fail. Period.

There are three parts of an action plan:

1. Planning Stage – typically occurs within the first six months of a business' initial start-up
2. Launch Stage – typically covers the business' first year of operation
3. Growth Stage –ongoing; however, it is important to have an exit strategy.[24]

Your action plan needs to clearly show how long each stage will last for your business, all the tasks that are associated with each stage, and how much each stage is going to cost. This allows you to determine when you must have funding in place

---

24 An exit strategy is how the entrepreneur plans to get out of the business. Viable exit strategies could be closing shop, selling the company, hiring a manager, or passing the business to the entrepreneur's children. It is important to have an end goal in mind for your business.

or where you might have to change your plan. Form 12 is provided to help you organize your plan to move forward.

Form 12   Action Plan

Stage	Timeframe	Tasks	Cost
Plan			
Launch			
Growth			

Action

Enough planning. Go, soar!

CONCLUSION

I think I should give the last word to my aforementioned friend and legal muse.

> At the beginning of January 2009 I was unemployed and looking for a job. While on the phone with Carla we discussed meeting for dinner and discussing the possibility of starting my own paralegal firm. This was something that I had wanted to do for a long time but had never known where to start. After only 2 hours, Carla was able to make sense of my business idea, crunch the numbers, and help me devise a plan of how to reach those numbers. In just under a month, I had one corporate client and 2 more pending. Carla's application of business models and enigmatic energy helped me to move forward with what I had always wanted to do. Last Friday I bought my first P.O. Box. I think that 2009 is going to be a good year!

Ally MacSporran

Paralegal and (New!) Small Business Owner

"Go! Go! Go!"

BIOGRAPHY

Growing up in the same house as an inventor meant that our basement was the factory, our kitchen the laboratory, and I a guinea pig. I've always been surrounded by good, bad and ugly ideas, but I didn't have the foundational know-how or the tools to properly distinguish between them – until I went back to school for my MBA.

I never thought that I'd write a book. Heck – I never thought that I'd live in China or Australia, that I'd teach part-time, or start my own business. But there are times when it just makes sense. Writing this book helped me to identify when the time was right for me to pursue my dream. I hope that it does the same for you.

My mantra is to enjoy the ride rather than to strive for the destination. You can't guarantee that you'll like where you end up. It's a whole lot easier to make sure that you like what you're doing now.